Intervening to Improve the Safety of Occupational Driving: A Behavior-Change Model and Review of Empirical Evidence

Intervening to Improve the Safety of Occupational Driving: A Behavior-Change Model and Review of Empirical Evidence has been co-published simultaneously as *Journal of Organizational Behavior Management*, Volume 19, Number 4 2000.

Intervening to Improve the Safety of Occupational Driving: A Behavior-Change Model and Review of Empirical Evidence

Timothy D. Ludwig, PhD
E. Scott Geller, PhD

Preface by
Thomas C. Mawhinney, PhD
Editor, *Journal of Organizational Behavior Management*

Intervening to Improve the Safety of Occupational Driving: A Behavior-Change Model and Review of Empirical Evidence has been co-published simultaneously as *Journal of Organizational Behavior Management*, Volume 19, Number 4 2000.

Routledge
Taylor & Francis Group
New York London

Intervening to Improve the Safety of Occupational Driving: A Behavior-Change Model and Review of Empirical Evidence has also been published as *Journal of Organizational Behavior Management,* Volume 19, Number 4 2000.

First published by
The Haworth Press, Inc., 10 Alice Street, Binghamton, NY 13904-1580 USA

This edition published 2012 by Routledge

Routledge
Taylor & Francis Group
711 Third Avenue
New York, NY 10017

Routledge
Taylor & Francis Group
2 Park Square, Milton Park
Abingdon, Oxon OX14 4RN

Cover design by Thomas J. Mayshock Jr.

Library of Congress Cataloging-in-Publication Data

Intervening to improve the safety of occupational driving: a behavior-change model and review of empirical evidence / Timothy D. Ludwig, E. Scott Geller, Thomas C. Mawhinney.

p. cm.

"Co-published simultaneously as Journal [of] organizational behavior management, volume 19, number 4 2000."

Includes bibliographical references and index.

ISBN 0-7890-1004-6 (alk. paper)–ISBN 0-7890-1012-7 (alk. paper)

1. Traffic accidents. 2. Delivery of goods. 3. Behavior modification. I. Ludwig, Timothy D. II. Geller, E. Scott, 1942-III. Mawhinney, Thomas C. IV. Journal of organizational behavior management.

HE5614.I586 2000
363.12′57–dc21

00-039602
CIP

ABOUT THE AUTHORS

Timothy D. Ludwig, PhD, is Associate Professor at Appalachian State University, where he directs the Industrial/Organizational Psychology master's program. He has over a dozen publications in applied behavior analysis focusing on occupational safety and other societal issues. He has chaired 7 symposia on behavioral safety research and presented in over 60 conference sessions. Dr. Ludwig's research has been cited in numerous textbooks including Kazdin (1994), Sarafino (1996), Lieberman (1999), and Spector (2000).

E. Scott Geller, PhD, is Professor of Psychology and Director of the Center for Applied Behavior Systems at Virginia Polytechnic Institute & State University, where he has been a faculty member since 1969. He is a Fellow of the American Psychological Association, the American Psychological Society, and the World Academy of Productivity and Quality. He is past Editor of *Journal of Applied Behavior Analysis* (1989-1992) and current Associate Editor (since 1983) of *Environment and Behavior.* He recently published his seventh book on managing behaviors and attitudes for occupational health and safety.

Intervening to Improve the Safety of Occupational Driving: A Behavior-Change Model and Review of Empirical Evidence

CONTENTS

Preface

AN INTEGRATIVE REVIEW OF SAFE DRIVING IMPROVEMENT INTERVENTIONS AMONG PIZZA DELIVERERS

In this volume, Timothy D. Ludwig and E. Scott Geller present a systematic review of their research which reveals the components and combinations of intervention techniques most likely to have salutary impacts on safe driving behavior. Selecting pizza delivery drivers as their target for the various interventions was no accident. As the authors are quick to point out, compared to other segments of the national driving population, this occupational group is at greater risk of being involved in unintentional car crashes that result in injuries to themselves and others. In addition, they exhibit an important characteristic found in the geneticists' favorite subject, the fruit fly. That is, cohorts of them enter and leave employment with pizza delivery operations fast enough that the same pizza operations can serve as research sites several times per year! Among other things, this relatively high rate of turnover among drivers permitted these researchers to collect data concerning whether safe driving practices fostered by an intervention with one cohort might be passed along as a "cultural practice" to the next cohort of drivers. Of even greater importance to scholars, researchers and practitioners concerned with identifying efficient and reliable means of promoting safer driving behavior among high risk drivers, the authors present evidence in support of their Multiple Intervention Level Model and Behavior Change Taxonomy. These two ways of organizing extant evidence concerning the causes and consequences of safety-related driving behavior provide a vantage point on ways of designing better interventions than would arise from a more haphazard approach. Together they help explain why and under what conditions an intervention aimed at changing one target

---

[Haworth co-indexing entry note]: "Preface." Mawhinney, Thomas C. Co-published simultaneously in *Journal of Organizational Behavior Management* (The Haworth Press, Inc.) Vol. 19, No. 4, 2000, pp. xiii-xiv; and: *Intervening to Improve the Safety of Occupational Driving: A Behavior-Change Model and Review of Empirical Evidence* (Timothy D. Ludwig and E. Scott Geller) The Haworth Press, Inc., 2001, pp. xi-xii. Single or multiple copies of this article are available for a fee from The Haworth Document Delivery Service [1-800-342-9678, 9:00 a.m. - 5:00 p.m. (EST). E-mail address: getinfo@haworthpressinc.com].

behavior will result in an ancillary change in another desired or undesired safe driving related behavior. The authors invoke the concepts of response and stimulus differentiation and generalization when offering their interpretation of the phenomena isolated in their work, i.e., concurrent increases and decreases in rates of behavior related to, but not the actual targets of, their interventions. Of equal importance, they report instances of apparent rule-governed behavior that has most of the earmarks of the phenomenon called countercontrol. The occurrence of countercontrol in the context of behavior based safety interventions is prima facie evidence that the participants experience the intervention contingencies as aversive as opposed to positively rewarding or "reinforcing." Empirical evidence organized by the authors in their MIL model and Behavior Change Taxonomy appears to predict, a priori, which components of an intervention and under what conditions they are likely to produce desirable instances of response generalization and undesirable instances of countercontrol. Both the behavioral concepts and field experimental methods used by these researchers are decidedly in the traditions of basic and applied behavior analysis. Those traditions support the matching of research methods that produce individual level data with behavioral concepts stated at the level of individual behavior. Researchers trained in other traditions, on the other hand, often use aggregated group data when evaluating individual level concepts. For example, countercontrol can be either an individual or a group level phenomenon. Therefore, the authors present data at both levels. Because response generalization is a process that occurs at the level of individual behavior, they present data at the group and individual level to clearly illustrate the importance of matching data to the level of the concept involved when evaluating evidence concerning such concepts. For all of these reasons scholars and researchers should find reading this work a rewarding experience. At the same time, practitioners seriously interested in learning how better to devise interventions that improve safe driving practices among professional drivers will find reading this work an equally rewarding and profitable experience. As the current editor of *JOBM,* I am simply delighted that the authors chose *JOBM* as the journal in which to place this very important review and rationalization of their long term research into safe driving behavior.

Thomas C. Mawhinney
Editor, Journal of Organizational Behavior Management

Intervening to Improve the Safety of Delivery Drivers: A Systematic Behavioral Approach

SUMMARY. This monograph reviews seven field studies that evaluated behavior-based interventions designed to increase safe-driving practices of pizza deliverers. Intervention strategies focused primarily on variations of goal-setting and feedback techniques, including: (a) non-numerical goals in an awareness and promise card intervention; (b) non-numerical goals mandated as company policy; (c) participative and assigned group goal setting paired with feedback; (d) group goal setting and feedback with added public individualized feedback; (e) individualized feedback and competition; and (f) private individualized feedback paired with dynamic, static, or dynamic and static goals. An additional intervention evaluated a community program in which pizza deliverers acted as behavior change agents for safety-belt use. Two models of intervention effectiveness were evaluated for their ability to help practitioners design interventions that maximize both short-term and long-term impacts as well as desirable response generalization. The amounts of individual involvement, peer support, response information, and external consequences influenced the beneficial impacts of the interventions. Additionally, maintenance of behavior change after the interventions were withdrawn varied directly with the degree of peer support and involvement in the interventions' designs. Employee involvement increased the amount of desirable response generalization while external consequences seemed to be associated with undesirable

---

Correspondence concerning this article should be addressed to Timothy D. Ludwig, Department of Psychology, Appalachian State University, 114 Smith-Wright Hall, Boone, NC 28608. Electronic mail may be sent via Internet to LUDWIGTD@APPSTATE.EDU.

[Haworth co-indexing entry note]: "Intervening to Improve the Safety of Delivery Drivers: A Systematic Behavioral Approach." Ludwig, Timothy D., and E. Scott Geller. Co-published simultaneously in *Journal of Organizational Behavior Management* (The Haworth Press, Inc.) Vol. 19, No. 4, 2000, pp. 1-124; and: *Intervening to Improve the Safety of Occupational Driving: A Behavior-Change Model and Review of Empirical Evidence* (Timothy D. Ludwig and E. Scott Geller) The Haworth Press, Inc., 2000, pp. 1-124. Single or multiple copies of this article are available for a fee from The Haworth Document Delivery Service [1-800-342-9678, 9:00 a.m. - 5:00 p.m. (EST). E-mail address: getinfo@haworthpressinc.com].

spread of effect presumed to be countercontrol.

KEYWORDS. Driving safety, goal setting, feedback, response generalization

Injury is the primary cause of lost-person-years of productive life in the U.S. (Waller, 1987a). Because of its prominence, the U.S. Department of Health and Human Services has identified injury prevention as a priority for attaining the goals outlined in *Healthy People 2000: National Health Promotion and Disease Prevention Objectives* (1991). Injuries from the estimated 6.8 million annual motor vehicle crashes account for approximately 45% of total unintentional injuries, including 41,907 deaths and approximately 3.5 million non-fatal injuries (National Highway Traffic Safety Administration, 1996). Thus, the national health objectives call for a reduction of deaths caused by motor vehicle crashes (Healthy People 2000 Objective 9.3; DHHS, 1991).

Injuries that occur on-the-job cost the U.S. economy an estimated $171 billion each year, and motor vehicle crashes are the leading cause of work-related deaths (National Center for Health Statistics, 1999). In addition, work-related motor vehicle crashes account for 22% of all workplace fatalities. These losses will surely increase as consumer demand for home or business delivery increases. For example, businesses already spend an estimated 18 billion dollars on courier delivery services (Niemira, 1998).

The home delivery of products is estimated to increase 16% annually. Internet shopping, where customers' product purchases are delivered to their homes, is already a 5.8 billion-dollar industry. Home delivery of food products continues to grow at a similar pace. One national pizza delivery corporation grew at a rate of 12.5% in 1997 with revenues of 1.04 billion dollars (Cravin, 1998). Therefore, the number of people who work in delivery-related jobs, whose primary task is driving on public roads, will continue to increase. Consequently, vehicle crashes represent a growing and significant health and productivity concern among delivery-oriented organizations.

Although many delivery-related workers are professionals with specialized driver training, some delivery jobs are performed by part-time workers. In the case of pizza delivery, these jobs are often held by individuals between the ages of 18 and 24, a specific demographic population particularly prone to unintentional injury by motor vehicle crashes. *Healthy People 2000* (1991) identifies motor vehicle crashes as the single leading cause of death among adolescents and young adults between the ages of 15 and 24, and has labeled this group a special target population for active intervention to reduce death and injury (Objective 9.3b). This report focuses on attempts to increase safe driving practices among people involved in part-time delivery work.

Pizza deliverers have a crash rate four times the national average. Numerous factors contribute to their excessive vehicle crash rate. First, pizza deliverers are part of an age group that has less experience driving and a disproportionate number of wrecks (National Center for Health Statistics, 1999). Therefore insurance companies assign their highest premiums to these individuals reflecting their higher risk. Second, these part-time workers often drive vehicles in need of safety-related maintenance, often as a result of excessive use from repeated deliveries. Third, the job often requires the deliverer to drive on town streets with numerous obstacles during the busiest and/or the most dangerous times of the day (e.g., "rush hour" and late evening). Fourth, the typical deliverer makes, on the average, 12 deliveries on a singe shift often without the breaks common to other jobs. Finally, pizza deliverers are typically compensated with a commission based on number of pizzas delivered. Tips to these deliverers are often based on the speed of their deliveries. Compensation systems of this type reward fast and efficient, yet often unsafe, driving practices.

BEHAVIOR-BASED INJURY REDUCTION

The antecedent-behavior-consequence model of applied behavior analysis has been used successfully over recent years to develop primary prevention programs. Indeed, behavior analysis has a great deal to offer the field of injury control. It can enhance prevention specialists' understanding of the determinants of injury-causing behaviors. Of equal importance, it can guide the development of effective behavior change strategies (e.g., Geller et al., 1990; Geller, 1988, 1996, 1997; Roberts et al., 1987; Sleet, Hollenbach, & Hovell, 1986).

Behavior-change research guided by the three-term contingency or A-B-C model has used: (a) *participative education* to increase vehicle safety-belt use (Cope, Smith, & Grossnickle, 1986; Geller, Rudd,

Kalsher, Streff, & Lehman, 1987; Weinstein, Grubb, & Vautier, 1986) and the acquisition of fire emergency skills (Jones, Ollendick, McLaughlin, & Williams, 1989); (b) *incentives/rewards* to increase the use of safety belts (Campbell, Hunter, & Stutts, 1984; Geller, 1984; Roberts, Fanurik, & Wilson, 1988) and child safety seats (Roberts & Fanurick, 1986); (c) *behavioral feedback* to decrease traffic crashes (Evans, 1991), reduce driving speed (Van Houten & Nau, 1983) and increase safety-belt use (Geller, 1996; Grant, 1990); (d) *promise-card commitment* to increase safety-belt use (Geller & Lehman, 1991; Kello, Geller, Rice, & Bryant, 1988; Geller, Kalsher, Rudd, & Lehman, 1989) and the use of personal protective equipment at industrial sites (Streff, Kalsher, & Geller, 1993); and (e) *modeling* to decrease alcohol-impaired driving and increase safety-belt use (Geller, 1990).

Malott (1992) distinguished between direct-acting contingencies, those that actually control behavior, and indirect-acting contingencies, those too remote to control behavior directly. Few safe driving behaviors are shaped by direct-acting contingencies. As Cerutti (1989) noted, "few drivers would survive learning to stop at red traffic lights if the discrimination could only be negatively reinforced by avoiding collisions" (p. 262). These consequences are too remote (e.g., delayed and/or improbable) to control behavior. Instead, most safe driving behaviors are under the influence of indirect-acting contingencies that often appear as rules that drivers are shaped to follow. Parents, governments, schools, and organizations create rules that offer more proximate three-term contingencies (Baum, 1994) such as traffic tickets or managerial action.

Safety-related rules are often promoted as part of an intervention. Interventions are systematic efforts to arrange environmental contexts so desired behavior is more likely to occur. Verbalizations by intervention agents (i.e., individuals who help deploy an intervention) take the form of instructions which describe correct performance and specify contingencies (Cerutti, 1989). Such instructions can influence behavior even in the absence of any sustained contact with the contingencies. Therefore, rule-governed behaviors are not necessarily shaped through associations with a contingency. Instead, interventions provide rules that specify the discriminated control of a stimulus, or a constellation of stimuli, over certain behaviors (as when a traffic light controls stopping behaviors). Some intervention techniques more effectively establish rules and behavior in compliance with rules than do others. In the following section two models aimed at helping predict intervention impact are presented and discussed.

INTERVENTION IMPACT MODELS

An intervention can have multiple effects. Some effects are defined and measured in order to ascertain whether the intervention was successful. Some effects are related to practical significance and determine the degree to which the problem was solved. We consider three criteria when evaluating the impact of a behavior-based safety intervention: (1) Did the target behavior change at some time during the intervention? (2) Did the target behavior sustain its improvement after withdrawal of the intervention? and (3) How did safety-related behaviors other than those targeted by the intervention change?

For the first criterion, we expect an intervention to have a "concurrent effect" on the targeted behavior. In past publications we called this criterion an immediate effect (Geller et al., 1990a). However, the direct impact of the intervention may not be observed immediately when the intervention begins. Although changes in the target behaviors occurred immediately after the intervention began in many of the studies reported in this monograph, sometimes a target behavior improved further as the intervention continued. In other studies substantial behavioral improvement did not occur until a couple of weeks into the intervention.

We refer to changes in the target behavior that occur at some time during the intervention as a *concurrent effect.* The concurrent effect is of particular concern to most researchers because it is a necessary step in demonstrating functional control of an intervention over the target behavior. Therefore, most methods of intervention evaluation include consideration of this criterion when assessing effectiveness of an intervention.

The second criterion used in assessment of an intervention's impact addresses the degree to which effects occurring during the intervention continue after the intervention has been terminated or removed from the setting. Stokes and Baer (1977) referred to this dimension as "generalization across time" putting it in the same category as generalization across settings or trainers. We call this second criterion of intervention impact a maintenance effect. The maintenance effect is assessed by continuing observations after the intervention operations have been removed. Even though the intervention operations have been removed from the setting, aspects of an intervention can still affect variables indigenous to the setting and help sustain the behavioral improvement. While the concurrent effect may be important to assess the functional control of an intervention, the maintenance effect often has more relevance to the participants and leaders held responsible for the target behavior at the field site.

Our third criterion for evaluating intervention impact considers behaviors other than those targeted by the intervention. In our opinion behavior analysts historically have taken too narrow a view of intervention impact. That is, most intervention researchers study one target response at a time. This practice makes it impossible to notice whether other responses covary as a function of shared functions or reinforcement histories. Indeed, an intervention may impact a number of behaviors similar to the target behavior in topography, form, or function (Skinner, 1953).

If an intervention effects improvement in more than the target behavior(s), we call it *response generalization.* In fact, interventions can result in either an increase or decrease in non-targeted safety-related behaviors. Response generalization (Bandura, 1969; Carr, 1988; Skinner, 1953) occurs when multiple behaviors that are functionally related to a common outcome (such as safe driving) increase as a result of intervening on one of the behaviors (Russo, Cataldo, & Cushing, 1981). On the other hand, an intervention process that relies heavily on external consequences might lead to countercontrol (Skinner, 1971) or opposing actions. In this case, an increase in a targeted behavior is associated with a decrease in a related but non-targeted behavior.

Models of Behavior Change

Over three decades of behavior change research led to our development and refinement of two models that applied researchers and practitioners can use to guide their design and evaluation of interventions. The *multiple intervention level* (MIL) hierarchy categorizes behavior change approaches with regard to their ability to influence behavior on a large scale. The *behavior change taxonomy* can guide the development of more effective behavior change techniques based on the three criteria of intervention impact described above (Geller et al., 1990a, 1990b; Geller & Ludwig, 1991; Geller, Needleman, & Randall, 1990).

The research reviewed here has important implications concerning validity of these two models for predicting the impact of interventions designed to increase safe driving.

A multiple intervention level (MIL) hierarchy. The multiple intervention level (MIL) hierarchy (as depicted in Figure 1) is characterized by dividing intervention strategies into multiple tiers, each defined by a level of intervention effectiveness, intensity, and cost. At the first or bottom level of the MIL hierarchy, the interventions are least intrusive and target the maximum number of people. At this level, the intervention is designed to have maximum large-scale appeal and minimum individual-to-individual contact, thereby resulting in the lowest overall cost per individual.

Repeated applications of similar interventions will be beneficial to individuals already affected by an initial intervention at that level (i.e., booster sessions). However, those individuals uninfluenced by the first exposure to a particular intervention will generally be uninfluenced by

FIGURE 1. The multiple intervention level (MIL) hierarchy.

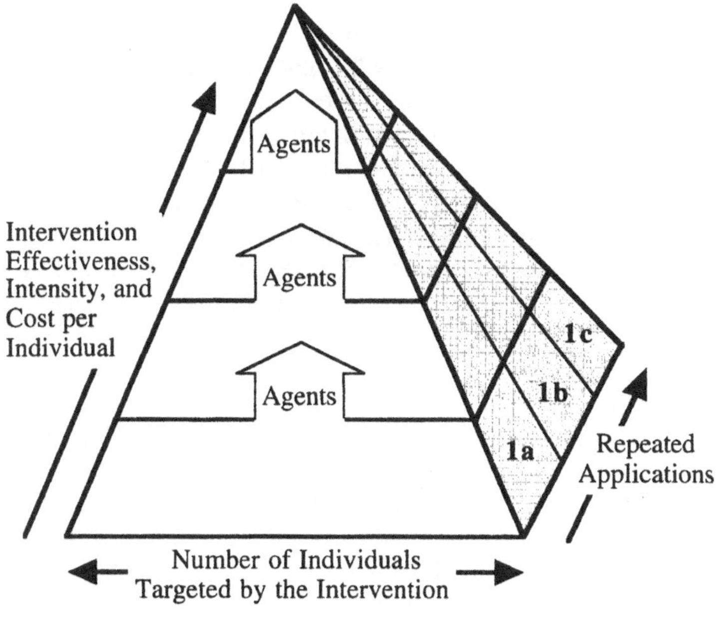

repeated exposure to interventions at the same level of intrusiveness. These individuals require a more intrusive, higher-level intervention.

The term intrusiveness has negative connotations. When a driver is stopped and ticketed for a traffic offense with the threat of a jail experience, this is an intrusive event in the life of the individual. However, higher-level interventions need not be bothersome or aversive. Instead, intrusiveness can also be conceptualized and, at some point operationalized, as an agent-to-participant ratio (Geller, Needleman, & Randall, 1990). With this ratio, the number of agents who are advocating change through the intervention is compared with the number of target individuals whom the intervention is intended to impact.

A lower-level intervention, as defined by the MIL model, is one with a lower agent-to-participant ratio. Public service radio or television announcements that advocate safe driving have only one or two agents for thousands of targets (or viewers) and are quite unintrusive or impersonal. Successively higher intervention levels are more costly and intrusive, but they are needed for the "hard core" problem individuals identified by their resistance to previous, lower-level interventions. These individuals are probably at greater risk of injury, both to themselves and, in the case of driving, to others.

Jessor (1987) and Melton (1988) have suggested those most difficult to reach with low-intrusive interventions are the persons most likely to emit behaviors that have the most damaging (or risky) consequences. For example, individuals most likely to drive in a risky or non-compliant manner (e.g., exceed speed limits and/or drive while intoxicated) are least likely to use safety belts (Evans, 1985; Hedlund, 1986). Belt use laws are rarely sufficient to get these individuals to buckle up, instead more intrusive or higher-level interventions are required.

The MIL model proposes that individuals influenced at a particular level of an intervention hierarchy become intervention agents for the next level of intervention (cf. Katz & Lazarfeld, 1955). Intervention programs that enlist individuals that already exhibit the desired behaviors, possibly as a result of a lower-level intervention, are able to increase the number of intervention agents available to intervene on problem individuals. This enables a higher agent-to-participant ratio and thus more intervention effectiveness.

Behavior Change Taxonomy. Table 1 depicts our most recent taxonomy of behavior change techniques for predicting intervention impact and for guiding the development of more effective intervention components. Geller (1998a) defined 26 different approaches to change behavior, distilled from the behavioral community psychology literature, especially publications in the *Journal of Organizational Behavior Management* and the *Journal of Applied Behavior Analysis* (cf. Greene et al., 1987). Some of the techniques occur before the target behavior and are considered antecedent procedures. Each represents an attempt to arrange conditions that increase the likelihood that a desired response will be emitted.

Feedback, rewards, and penalties are environmental events that can be delivered or withheld contingent on occurrences of a behavior (e.g., depressing a brake pedal to come to a complete stop) or the outcomes of a behavior (e.g., traffic citations and vehicle crashes resulting from at-risk driving). Rewards include pleasing items or events as well as opportunities to escape or avoid unpleasant situations. Penalties, on the other hand, typically involve the presentation of an unpleasant event (e.g., a jail term or requirement to do community service) or the removal of a pleasant item or privilege (e.g., money or a driver's license).

The taxonomy in Table 1 also distinguishes between behavior change techniques that target the behavior of individuals versus groups. Research reviewed in this monograph, among other things, compared the impact of goal-setting and feedback techniques as applied to individuals versus groups. Brief definitions of the 26 behavior change techniques listed in Table 1 appear in Geller (1998a).

According to the behavior change taxonomy, four factors contribute to intervention impact (including concurrent and maintained effects, as well as response generalization). Based on our review of empirical studies of injury prevention (see Geller, 1998a), we contend that an intervention's effectiveness is a function of the amount of: (a) individual *involvement* facilitated by the intervention, (b) *peer support* promoted by intervention procedures, (c) *response information* transmitted by the intervention, and (d) *external consequences* implicated by the intervention.

Involvement is defined by the amount of intervention-related behavioral activity or participation among individuals whose behavior is targeted by the intervention. Involvement is presumed to vary as a function of the agent-to-participant ratio (i.e., the greater the number

TABLE 1. The Behavior Change Taxonomy

Behavior Change Techniques	Involvement	Peer Support	Response Information	External Consequences	Concurrent Impact	Maintained Impact	Generalized Effect
1. Lecture	0	0	1	0	1	0	0
2. Demonstration	0	1	1	0	2	1	0
3. Policy	0	0	1	1	2	0	−1
4. Commitment	1	0	1	0	2	1	1
5. Discussion/Consensus	1	1	1	0	3	2	1
6. Intervention Agent	1	1	1	0	3	2	1
7. Written Activator	0	0	1	0	1	0	0
8. Oral Activator	0	1	1	0	2	1	0
9. Assigned Individual Goal	0	0	1	1	2	0	−1
10. Personal Goal	1	0	1	0	2	1	1
11. Individual Competition	0	0	1	1	2	0	−1
12. Individual Incentive	1	0	1	1	3	1	0
13. Individual Disincentive	1	0	1	1	3	1	0
14. Individual Feedback	0	0	1	1	2	0	−1
15. Individual Reward	0	0	1	1	2	0	−1
16. Individual Penalty	0	0	1	1	2	0	−1
17. Self-Observation	1	0	1	0	2	1	1
18. Self-Reward	1	0	1	0	2	1	1
19. Assigned Group Goal	0	1	1	1	3	1	−1
20. Participative Group Goal	1	1	1	0	3	2	1
21. Group Competition	0	1	1	1	3	1	−1
22. Group Incentive	0	1	1	1	3	1	−1
23. Group Disincentive	0	1	1	1	3	1	−1
24. Group Feedback	0	1	1	1	3	1	−1
25. Group Reward	0	1	1	1	3	1	−1
26. Group Penalty	0	1	1	1	3	1	−1

<u>Concurrent Impact</u> = Involvement + Peer Support + Response Information + External Consequences

<u>Maintained Impact</u> = Involvement + Peer Support

<u>Generalized Effect</u> = Involvement − External Consequences

of change agents per target population the greater the individual involvement). We contend that involvement in an intervention creates an association between the contingencies provided by the intervention and the establishing operations (or EOs; Michael, 1982) in the occupational setting. In addition, involvement in an intervention may allow individuals to arrange an environment to support the maintenance of the targeted behavior. Employee involvement can shape rule-governed behavior that is self-reinforcing and maintained not only by the intervention but by the occupational setting itself. Therefore, we expect involvement to be a critical factor when considering response maintenance and response generalization.

Peer support is a function of the degree of coworker interaction facilitated by the intervention. Peer support can take the form of social reinforcers or punishers as well as interpersonal prompting. Interventions high in peer support provide a setting in which social reinforcers from other individuals (e.g., family, friends, work groups) are a likely consequence for the desired behavior. Peer support helps maintain increases in the targeted behavior(s) when the formal intervention process is withdrawn.

Response information varies directly with the amount of three-term contingency specifics provided by an intervention. This can be facilitated by increasing the salience of the information relevant to the context and the individual, as well as the temporal proximity between a behavioral request and the opportunity for compliance (cf. Geller, Winett, & Everett, 1982).

This factor is difficult to judge, however, because the amount of response information depends upon the particular message conveyed by the intervention, the program recipient's prior knowledge of the target behavior, and whether behavior-based feedback was available. For example, written activators (such as signs or memos that specify desired behaviors) are often informative during an initial exposure. However, after viewers become aware of the appropriate response, the same activator conveys less information, essentially serving only as a reminder. Thus, while lectures, discussions, and demonstrations may provide new response information for some individuals, they are merely reminders for others. An antecedent must offer new information (e.g., through behavioral feedback) in order to continue to have an informational impact beyond that produced by its first presentation.

Interventions high in external consequences manipulate a response consequence (i.e., a reward or penalty) in order to influence a target behavior. We expect external consequences to have a strong influence on the concurrent effects of an intervention. The term "external" is used here to imply that these consequences are not indigenous to the work setting and are usually contrived (Geller, 1996). Therefore, they are not expected to influence behavioral maintenance after their termination. Moreover, we expect that strong external consequences may differentiate (Catania, 1979) the targeted behavior to the point of limiting response generalization. In fact, if external consequences are delivered in a manner that is controlling (as implied by the term "behavior modification"), countercontrol may occur (Skinner, 1971).

The taxonomy attempts to score each behavior change technique according to its facilitation of involvement and peer support, and its provision of response information and external contingencies. To derive the factor scores for each behavior change technique, we first defined each behavior change procedure according to recent applications of behavior analysis aimed at promoting health and safety. Then we judged whether the procedures and operations inherent in a behavior change technique included aspects of the evaluation factors. Currently, a simple all-or-none (present = 1, absent = 0) point system is used to indicate whether a behavior change technique has attributes consistent with the particular factor. Factor points are summed to produce a score for concurrent impact. Maintained impact and response generalization scores are computed by summing the factor points and subtracting points for external consequences.

Our aim is to generate a more sensitive scoring scheme based on empirical tests of the various behavior change techniques. For example, differential observations of involvement and peer support across different intervention techniques (e.g., "Lecture" or "Demonstration" vs. "Discussion/Consensus") suggest ratings of "degree" rather than "all-or-none." The research described in this monograph was designed in part to test certain aspects of the Behavior Change Taxonomy.

We argue that interventions aimed at controlling behavior by an external agent using rewards, surveillance, penalties and the like differ from those that involve potential participants in defining their own contingencies or establishing operations. Some of the research reviewed here tested whether involvement at some stage of the intervention was an important component in the maintenance of long-term behavior change, and whether involvement can lead to positive changes in safety behaviors not directly targeted by an intervention. This issue is of particular importance for injury prevention because interventions that target a single behavior, but have indirect beneficial effects on other desired behaviors, will be particularly cost effective.

SEVEN STUDIES TARGETING PIZZA DELIVERERS

Participants

Pizza deliverers were observed departing for and arriving from their deliveries over a ten-year span of systematic field experiments. The mean age of the deliverers was 23.3 years, ranging from 19 to 44, and their mean education was about 2 years of college. All deliverers worked on commission (per total pizzas sold), which averaged approximately $.58 per delivery plus gratuity at the beginning and $.75 per delivery plus gratuity at the end of our studies.

Because the turnover rate of pizza deliverers was about 75%, cohorts of deliverers turned over relatively completely every 4 to 6 months, it was possible to apply different intervention strategies in the same locations every 6 months or so. Also, pizza deliverers made up to 12 deliveries per shift and often worked 3 to 7 shifts a week. Thus, when a number of deliverers were on duty, it was not uncommon for observers to record data from 75 to 150 behavioral incidents in a two-hour session. This was especially true when observations were made during peak business hours, which were dinner and lunch hours and from 9:00 to 11:00 p.m. at night. For the 7 studies reviewed here, the average number of observations was 77 per observation session.

Setting

Eight pizza delivery stores from four different towns participated as either experimental or control sites although not all stores were used in each study. All stores had parking lots connected to two-way streets that had a speed limit of 35 mph. Three of the stores were located in a town of 35,000 in northwest North Carolina (NC) which included a medium-sized university serving 13,000 students. These stores were franchises of three different national pizza companies that offer delivery. One NC store shared a parking lot with two other businesses that had two exits onto two-lane roads. The second NC store shared a parking lot with one other business that had two exits onto a four-lane road. The third NC store had one exit onto a four-lane road. All three stores were within one mile of a state university serving 13,000 students.

Five additional stores were located in three towns in southwest Virginia. These stores represented the same three national chains as the stores in NC. Three stores were from one town with a population of 50,000. Two of these two stores had exits onto a four-lane road, and the other shared a parking lot with one other business that had one exit onto a two-lane road. All three of these stores were within one mile of a state university serving 25,000 students. One store in an adjacent town with a population of 40,000 also was within a mile of a state university serving 14,000 students. It had a parking lot exiting onto a four-lane road. The final store was located in a town with a population of 30,000 with no university and had a parking lot exiting onto a two-lane road. The parking lots from all stores were connected to roads posting a 35 mph speed limit. Additionally, behavioral observations of civilians (i.e., non-pizza deliverers) were conducted at all observation sites.

Dependent Measures

The dependent variables targeted for change in the research reviewed here include behavioral deficits (turn-signal use, complete intersection stopping, and safety-belt use) that contribute substantially to injuries and fatalities from vehicle crashes. During peak business hours (i.e., dinner time, 5:00-8:00 p.m.; lunch time, 11:30-1:30 p.m.; and evening, 9:00 p.m.-11:00 p.m.), behavioral observations were unobtrusively recorded by trained research assistants from windows of nearby businesses overlooking the pizza stores' parking lots. Observations were recorded using a checklist format our research team had used during more than ten years of observing pizza deliverers.

Behavioral observations were made when the pizza deliverer entered and exited the stores' parking lots. Observers recorded whether each pizza deliverer was using the available safety-belt shoulder strap (i.e., safety-belt use). They also recorded which direction the deliverer turned (i.e., turn direction), and whether the right or left turn signal was used (i.e., turn-signal use). For some studies, the observer also recorded whether the vehicle stopped completely before entering the main road from the intersection near each store (i.e., intersection stopping). At the time of the intersection observation, data collectors also recorded the traffic conditions the driver confronted when entering the main road. A simple binary (yes-no) estimate was recorded to indicate whether the oncoming traffic could have affected the deliverer's stopping behavior.

During most observations, the license plate number of the vehicle was recorded. To increase the ease and accuracy of identifying the license plate numbers, sheets containing descriptions of each pizza deliverer's vehicle and the corresponding license number were compiled for each store and used during the behavioral observations. By designing the data collection process to record license plate numbers, individual deliverers were tracked over the course of a study and even across several studies. This ability to track individuals allowed us to study patterns of individual compliance with a particular intervention. We limited data analysis to only those deliverers who had been observed more than 6 times per each phase in a given study. This process assured we had obtained ample baseline observations for each individual, and that each driver was observed sufficiently in all experimental phases.

Interobserver Reliability

For approximately one third of the observation sessions, interobserver reliability data were collected by a core of trained research assistants. During reliability sessions, two observers collected data concurrently at a single store. They were instructed not to confer about their observations, except to verify that they were observing the same vehicle.

Inter-observer reliability is calculated by comparing each individual record on the checksheet and calculating the percent of times the two observers agreed on specific events. Overall reliability (or percentage agreement) was 93% for safety-belt use (ranging from 88% to 100% agreement), 89% for turn-signal use (ranging from 78% to 100% agreement), and 88% for complete stops (ranging from 82% to 94% agreement).

Goal-Setting and Feedback Interventions

Table 2 outlines the various goal-setting and feedback interventions evaluated and lists the target behaviors, methodological design, and

TABLE 2. Characteristics of Seven Studies Targeting the Driving Practices of Pizza Deliverers

Study	Name of Intervention	Targeted Behavior(s)	Design	Behavior Change Techniques	Amount of Involvement	Amount of Peer Support	Amount of Response Information	Amount of External Consequences
Ludwig & Geller (1991)	Awareness and Promise Cards	Safety-Belt Use	ABA multiple baseline across settings with comparison group	• Commitment • Discussion/Concensus • Written Activator	High	High	Moderate	Low
Ludwig & Geller (1999a)	Policy	Turn-Signal Use	ABB' multiple baseline across settings	• Policy • Written Activator	Low	Low	Low	Moderate
Ludwig & Geller (1997)	Participative Group Goal Setting and Feedback	Complete Intersection Stopping	ABA multiple baseline across two different interventions with comparison group	• Discussion/Concensus • Written Activator • Team Goal • Group Feedback	High	High	Moderate	Low
	Assigned Group Goal Setting and Feedback	Complete Intersection Stopping		• Lecture • Written Activator • Assigned Group Goal • Group Feedback	Low	Moderate	Moderate	High
Ludwig, Geller, & Clarke (1999)	Group Goal Setting and Feedback	Turn-Signal Use	ABCA multiple baseline across settings with multiple comparison groups	• Written Activator • Team Goal • Group Feedback	Moderate	High	Moderate	Low
	Public Individual Feedback Added	Turn-Signal Use		Add • Individual Feedback	Low	High	High	Low
Ludwig, Briggs, Wagner, & Geller (1999)	Individual Competition with Rewards	Turn-Signal Use or Complete Intersection Stopping	ABA multiple baseline across settings and behaviors with multiple comparison groups	• Written Activator • Individual Feedback Reward • Individual Competition	Low	Low	High	High
Ludwig, Briggs, & Reynolds (1998)	Static, Dynamic, Static/Dynamic Individual Goal Setting and Feedback	Turn-Signal Use	Random assignment to groups in an ABA design	• Written Activator • Assigned Individual Goal • Individual Feedback	Low	Low	High	High
Ludwig & Geller (1999b)	Community Agents	Safety-Belt Use	ABA design with a comparison group	• Intervention Agent • Written Activators	High	High	Moderate	Low

the relation of the intervention program to the behavior change taxonomy (Table 1). The studies reviewed below demonstrate systematic research testing the impact of different goal-setting and feedback processes. One intervention strategy included neither goal setting nor feedback, but permitted evaluation of other techniques suggested by the Behavior Change Taxonomy (i.e., intervention-agent recruitment).

Arguably, goals can be conceived of as rules that govern the behavior they target if both goals and rules are defined as contingency specifying statements that have function altering effects on three-term (A-B-C) environmental contingencies. To function as rules, as defined by Blakely and Schlinger (1987; Schlinger & Blakely, 1987), goals statements must be effective (i.e., they must precipitate a change in the goal-related behavior). Goals statements typically refer to what Baum (1994) called ultimate contingencies and Malott (1992) has called indirect acting contingencies (e.g., "safer driving practices reduce accidents and injuries"). When goals and rules have an impact on behavior it is because they activate what Baum (1994) calls proximate three-term contingencies and Malott (1992) calls direct acting three-term contingencies.

The goals in many of our interventions: (a) were statements that specified a small proximate contingency (e.g., behavior-reward or B-C contingency) as well as implied a greater consequence, albeit less likely to be experienced, within an ultimate contingency (i.e., involvement in a vehicle crash); (b) designated antecedent environmental stimuli intended to function as behavioral prompts (e.g., feedback signs and managerial observations); and (c) were prescriptions for correct performance (i.e., a turn-signal use policy). When effective, these verbal descriptions of proximate and ultimate contingencies are instances of rules as defined by Blakely and Schlinger (Schlinger & Blakely, 1987; Blakely & Schlinger, 1987).

Feedback can be presented in a number of ways and can target individuals or groups (usually naturally-occurring groups like a certain work team or a whole shift of employees). Feedback can be delivered to a group without any corresponding goal. For example, Komaki, Heinemann, and Lawson (1980) posted group feedback to improve safety among employees in a city's vehicle maintenance division, and Fellner and Sulzer-Azaroff (1984) provided frequent group feedback to employees in a paper mill. Locke and Latham (1980) and Pritchard et al. (1988) suggested that when feedback is introduced in the absence of overt goal setting such as in these studies and others by Komaki, Collins and Penn (1982), Pritchard et al. (1988) and Sarri, (1987), "implicit" personal goal setting occurs spontaneously.

When goal setting is added to a feedback strategy, the target behavior(s) are not only defined, but a desired frequency of the behavior(s) is also specified. After a group feedback condition, Fellner and Sulzer-Azaroff (1985) added goal-setting conditions in a paper mill. Reber and Wallin (1984) assigned farm machinery manufacturing employees specific and difficult goals, and delivered departmental feedback in relation to their goals. Cooper, Phillips, Sutherland, and Makin (1994) allowed British construction workers to participate in their goal setting and gave them posted weekly departmental safety feedback.

In nearly every case, except for Fellner and Sulzer-Azaroff (1985), group goal setting paired with group feedback was effective, i.e., frequency of safety-related behavior increased. Locke and Latham (1990) concluded, after reviewing numerous studies beyond the safety literature, that goal setting and feedback together were more effective than either goal setting or feedback alone. These conclusions reflect those of Erez (1977) who demonstrated empirically that feedback is a necessary moderator for goal setting, and with another review of the literature by Balcazar, Hopkins, and Suarez (1986).

Our taxonomy helped organize our evaluation of a number of different goal-setting and feedback combinations. We varied our application of goal-setting and feedback using several different procedures. First, we varied the degree of goal specificity. In the first two studies, goals were established but no specific numerical targets were stated. In contrast, another study provided individuals with individualized numerical goals and feedback using percentages to specify the gap between an ultimate goal and an individual's performance.

Second, we varied the organizational level of goal setting and feedback, making the goal applicable to a group in some settings and to individuals in others. Other studies provided both group and individualized feedback. Third, we varied the amount of involvement the employees had during the intervention. Some studies used strong external consequences like mandated goals and policies, whereas others allowed employees to set the goal, choose rewards, and/or discuss the benefits of targeting certain behaviors.

Six of our studies included some kind of goal-setting and feedback manipulation. Table 3 is a matrix into which the six studies have been organized based on goal-setting manipulations (down the rows) and feedback procedures used (across columns at the top). Goal setting was presented to either groups of deliverers in a store or to individuals. Also included is a condition that did not provide a numerical goal.

Feedback was based on either group or individual behavior. Furthermore, individual feedback was divided into two categories of public or private distribution. A final category represents a condition where no feedback was provided. Certainly other factors such as design, behavior targeted, amount of participation, and frequency of feedback could be considered when contrasting the studies reviewed here. These factors are considered below when summarizing the results of the studies within the context of the Behavior Change Taxonomy.

TABLE 3. Goal Setting and Feedback Features of Intervention Programs

Type of Goal	Type of Feedback			
	Group	Individual Public	Individual Private	None
Group	Ludwig & Geller (1997): Participation vs. Assigned Goal Setting Ludwig, Geller, & Clarke (1999): 1st Intervention with Group Goal Setting and Group Feedback	Ludwig, Geller, & Clarke (1999): 2nd Intervention Adding Individual Feedback		
Individual			Biggs, Ludwig, & Reynolds (1998): Static vs. Dynamic Goal Setting	
Competition		Ludwig, Biggs, Wagner, & Geller (1999): Feedback with Competition		
Group, Non-numerical				Ludwig & Geller (1991): Awareness and Promise Card Ludwig & Geller (1999): Policy

The first study evaluated the impact of a group interactive awareness session among pizza deliverers that focused on the value of using vehicle safety belts (Ludwig & Geller, 1991). The second study tested the effects of a specific organizational policy (Ludwig & Geller, 1999a). The third study (Ludwig & Geller, 1997) contrasted a participative goal-setting intervention with assigned goal-setting. The fourth study (Ludwig, Geller, & Clarke, 1999) examined the impact of group feedback with additional public individual feedback in the context of a group goal. The fifth study (Ludwig, Biggs, Wagner, & Geller, 1999) added individual rewards to the public individual feedback intervention. The sixth study (Ludwig, 1999) contrasted static and dynamic goal-setting with individual private feedback. The final study explored the efficacy of a community safety-belt program using pizza deliverers as intervention agents to increase the use of safety-belts by both the pizza deliverers and the public at large (Ludwig & Geller, 1999b).

AWARENESS SESSIONS AND PROMISE CARDS (LUDWIG & GELLER, 1991)

In our first intervention project with pizza deliverers, we used an established method of behavior change to test our methodology in this unique field setting. Geller et al. (1987) reviewed five corporate safety-belt studies that applied an interactive small-group discussion format. These programs began with a 20 to 25-minute group discussion followed by the signing of pledge cards indicating individual commitment to buckle up. After comparing these studies with 13 studies using reward procedures, Geller et al. concluded there was consistently more maintenance of safety-belt use with the non-reward interventions.

The Target Behavior

This initial study targeted the safety-belt use of pizza deliverers at two stores. The use of shoulder and lap belts is the single most protective behavior that can be conveniently performed to reduce the risk of death or injury in a vehicle crash. In fact, it is estimated that 55% of all fatalities and 65% of all injuries from vehicle crashes would be prevented if safety belts were used. According to one estimate, a mere 10% increase in safety-belt use would prevent as many as 30,000 injuries and save 1,500 lives and $800 million in direct costs (Sleet, 1987).

The Intervention

The intervention we developed for this study used the Discussion/Consensus and Commitment techniques from the taxonomy. These techniques offer involvement, peer support and response information. From the taxonomy we would expect this intervention to have both concurrent and maintenance impact as well as demonstrate response generalization.

The intervention program was staggered across two pizza stores in multiple baseline fashion. During a group meeting, the facilitator and manager followed a script that prompted employees to discuss the value of safety-belts and strategies they could use to remember to buckle up. During this session a consensus was reached that the general public paid particular attention to their driving behavior because they were semi-professional drivers working for a highly publicized company. Following this discussion, drivers were presented with feedback regarding their low safety-belt use.

The employees were then asked if safety-belt use should be a goal for the group, and they agreed. However, no numerical level of performance was associated with the goal. This type of goal with no numerical benchmark has been called a "do your best" goal by Locke and Latham (1990) and they used it this way in some studies. However, others contend that a "goal" without a specified level to shoot for is not really a goal (Geller, 1994, 1996).

Finally, individuals were asked to make a personal commitment by signing a buckle-up promise card (Geller & Lehman, 1991). Subsequently, employee-designed buckle-up reminder signs were placed in the pizza stores, and the pizza cooks reminded the deliverers to "buckle-up" as they left the store. After the intervention ended the signs were taken down.

Results

During baseline, safety-belt use was quite low, indicating we had chosen an appropriate behavior to target. Absence of a ceiling effect increased the likelihood the intervention could produce dramatic results. Data plotted in Figure 2 show that the use of safety belts increased substantially above baseline at both intervention stores. Specifically, safety-belt use at Stores A and B increased respectively from baseline means of 41% and 14% to 68% and 69% during the interventions at each store.

The impact of the awareness meeting itself is apparent in the immediate and substantial increase in safety-belt use on the day of this session for Store A and for Store B. After the reminder signs were removed, safety-belt use continued at a high level (mean usage being 69% and 41% at Stores A and B, respectively). Thus, maintenance of intervention impact was evident for at least 3 months.

Kazdin (1973) argued that showing a reversal to baseline levels is fundamental in demonstrating functional control of the target behavior. However, in this study a total reversal was neither expected nor desired. Therefore, to demonstrate intervention impact, we had to rely on a multiple baseline design with a nonequivalent comparison group. No changes were observed among comparison groups in either safety-belt or turn-signal use over the course of the 7-month study.

Baer, Wolf, and Risley (1968) characterized intervention durability

FIGURE 2. Percent weekly safety-belt use across baseline, intervention, and follow-up phases at Stores A, B, and C during Ludwig and Geller (1991). Vertical lines around data points represent the range of daily safety-belt use during that week.

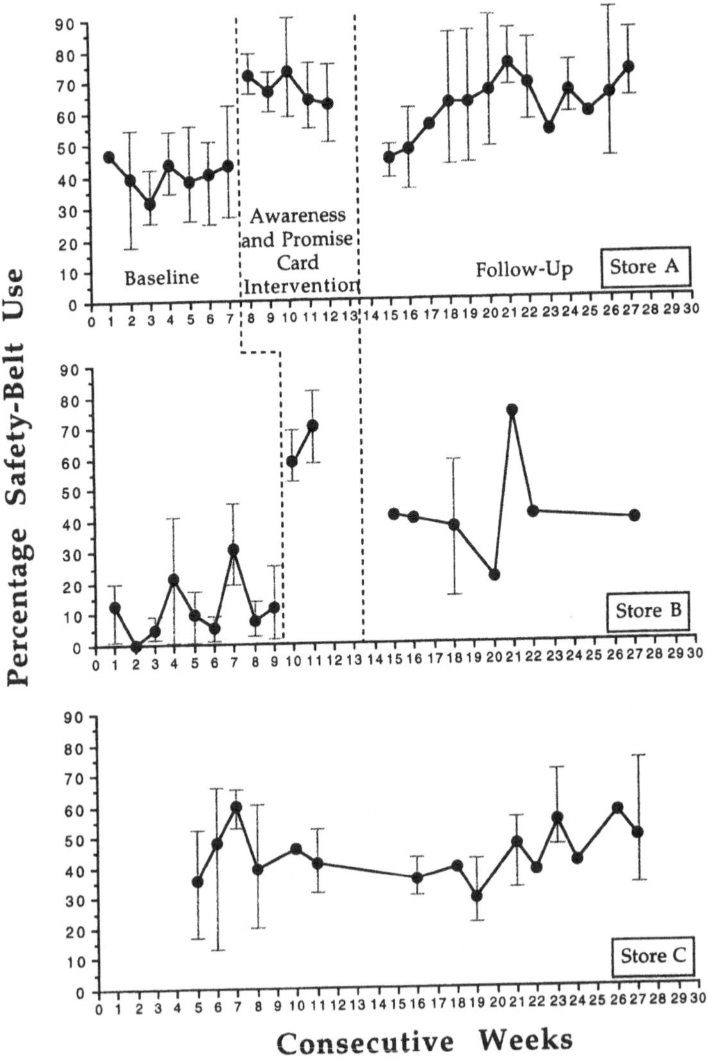

as behavior change that is maintained over time, even when the treatment is withdrawn. This, according to Baer et al., should be one of the goals of an applied approach to behavior analysis. The awareness and promise-card intervention prompted the use of indigenous peer support within the stores. Also, while we could remove the reminder signs, we could withdraw neither the individual rule-governed behavior precipitated by their public pledges, changes in individuals' verbal behavior (e.g., saying "buckle-up" as deliverers departed), nor the changes in various other cultural practices effected by the intervention.

Since license plate numbers were recorded during data collection, so we were able to track individual pizza deliverers before, during, and after the intervention program. We found, not surprisingly, significant diversity in the deliverers' reactions to the intervention. Data plotted in Figure 3 show the patterns of safety-belt use across five deliverers before and during the intervention. Some deliverers responded to the intervention as anticipated, going from a low baseline level to a higher frequency of safety-belt use during the intervention. Other drivers were unresponsive to the intervention program.

Other interesting patterns emerged. One deliverer's (#013) safety-belt use was high at the beginning of baseline observations. A check revealed that this deliverer had just started working with the company. His safety-belt use declined dramatically at one point during baseline, suggesting that some establishing operation might have occurred in the store to actually discouraged safety-belt use. For example, he might have noticed that other drivers were delivering pizzas quicker and making more money because of shortcuts they were taking, including not using a safety belt. This individual's safety-belt use returned to its previous level after he attended the intervention meeting with his coworkers. This suggests that if there had been a cultural practice of avoiding safety-belt use prior to the intervention, it was replaced by a cultural practice that supported safety-belt use following the intervention. This interpretation of the data is congruent with the fact that the increased safety-belt use produced by the intervention endured beyond the intervention phase.

Finally, one deliverer (#007) exhibited a fundamentally different pattern of behavior. This deliverer used his safety-belt nearly 100% of the time before the intervention. However, during the intervention his safety-belt use dropped to near 0% and remained low throughout the

FIGURE 3. Percent weekly safety-belt use of five deliverers at Store A before and during the Ludwig and Geller (1991) awareness intervention.

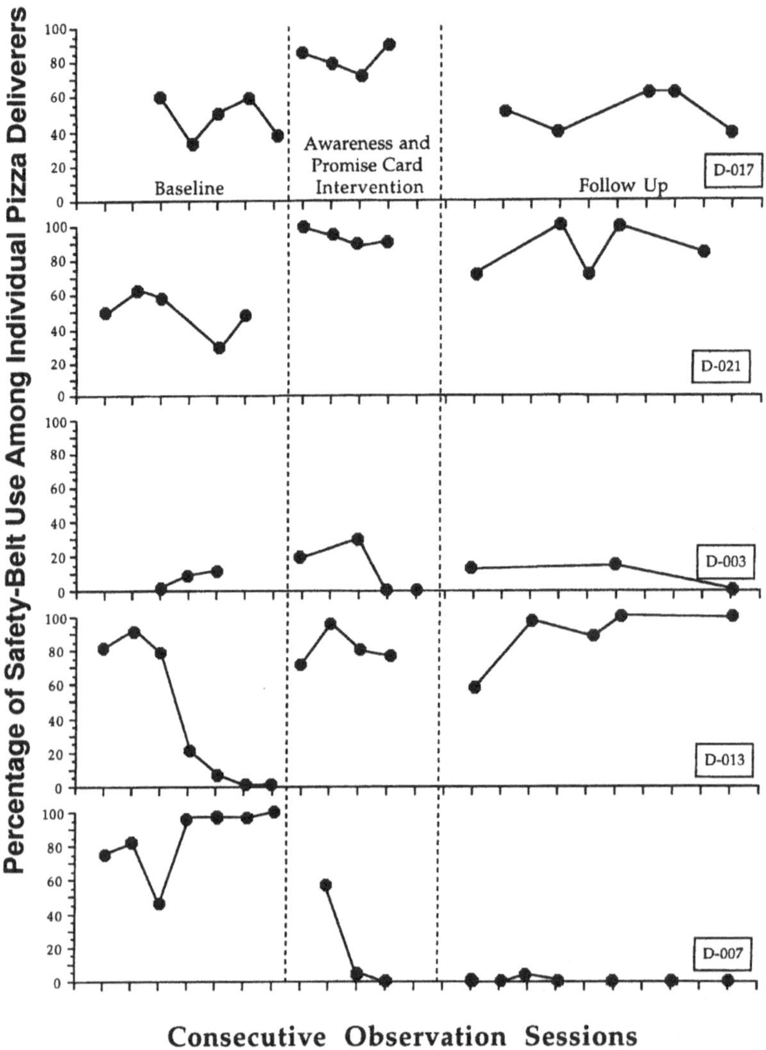

remainder of the study (see Panel 5 of Figure 3). Unfortunately we missed the opportunity to interview this individual to find out why his behavior declined so dramatically.

Examination of response patterns participant-by-participant and comparing them to the aggregated data for their respective groups yields an important lesson regarding effects of data aggregation on conclusions. While they are useful for summarizing the average impact of an intervention across members of a group, averaging data across many individuals masks response patterns that could be extremely instructive in learning more about effective intervention design and continuous improvement.

Linking license plate numbers to individual driving records permitted us to examine certain aspects of driving history as potential moderators of pre-and post-intervention belt use. Data plotted in Figure 4 show pre-and post-intervention safety-belt use grouped by driving history variables. Baseline belt use was significantly lower among drivers with one or more driving demerits or crashes during the previous five years. During the intervention program, however, these "risky" drivers increased their belt use to the same level as drivers with no demerits or crashes.

Although safety-belt use was similar for younger (under 25) and older (25 or older) drivers during baseline, younger drivers were markedly more responsive to the intervention than older drivers. Individual variation in belt use during baseline, intervention, and follow-up phases indicated that some drivers required more effective and costly intervention programs than those offered by their community (e.g., traffic laws, driver training, and public service announcements) to motivate their safe-driving practices. The MIL model predicts that this type of intervention, with a higher agent-to-participant ratio and more intrusive operations (e.g., commitment cards) will be more successful in influencing this segment of the population.

Generalization Effects

Our examination of a non-target behavior (i.e., turn-signal use) was inspired by Willems' (1974, 1977) contention that applied behavior analysts need to adopt a more ecological approach, as well as brief discussions about the notion of response generalization by Kazdin (1973) and others (Carr, 1988; Skinner, 1953; Sulzer-Azaroff & Mayer, 1991). Data plotted in Figure 5 show the turn-signal use of the

FIGURE 4. Percent safety-belt use across the baseline and intervention phases during Ludwig and Geller (1991) as a function of driving history.

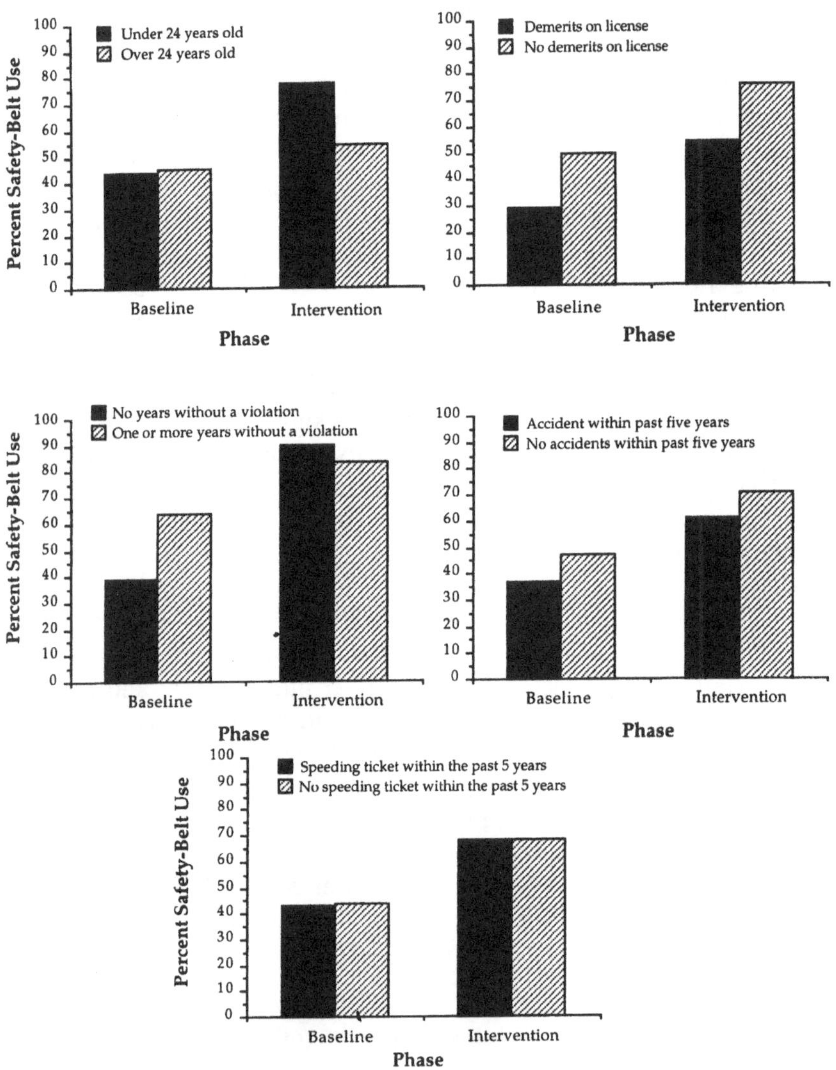

pizza deliverers over the course of this study. Turn-signal use at Store A increased from a baseline of 58% to 74% during the safety-belt intervention. Similarly, turn-signal use at Store B increased from a baseline of 40% to 49% during the intervention.

Thus, during an intervention targeting safety-belt use, mean turn-signal use rose by 25% relative to baseline. An analysis of the videotape created during the group meeting verified that group members never mentioned nor discussed turn-signal use. Evidently, the effect of the intervention spread to another behavior similar to the targeted behavior. We considered this an instance of response generalization and planned additional studies specifically designed to investigate this phenomenon systematically.

The awareness intervention study used a non-numerical group goal paired with signing a promise card. The intervention process facilitated much employee involvement. In contrast, the next study investigated the impact of a mandated store policy implemented with no employee involvement. More specifically, the management at two pizza stores mandated a policy that required all employees to signal their vehicle turns. Thus, degree of employee involvement in the development of a behavior-based intervention was the primary distinction between interventions in the first two studies reviewed here.

A MANDATED TURN-SIGNAL USE POLICY (LUDWIG & GELLER, 1999a)

From the standpoint of the behavior change taxonomy, a policy statement represents an intervention that rarely involves employees or solicits peer support. Instead policy statements rely on real and implied external consequences such as managerial penalties. According to the taxonomy, policy statements are expected to have a marginal immediate impact, affect only the safest individuals, and have little long-term impact.

Intervention

Turn-signal use was mandated among pizza deliverers at two stores (Ludwig & Geller, 1999a). Store managers created a policy statement that read: "It is the policy of (*name of franchise*) that all drivers use

FIGURE 5. Percent weekly turn-signal use across baseline, intervention, and follow-up phases at Stores A, B, and C during Ludwig and Geller (1991). Vertical lines around data points represent the range of daily safety-belt use during that week.

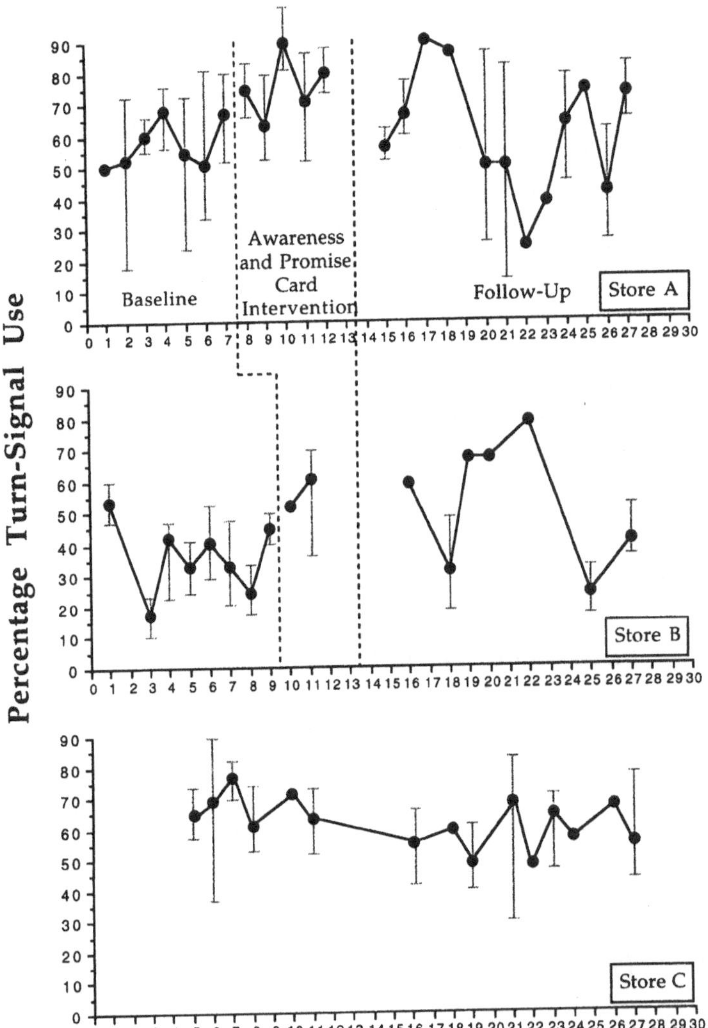

their turn signal at every intersection when making a delivery." This statement was printed on pink paper and attached to each deliverer's paycheck for two consecutive pay periods delivered two weeks apart.

Results

Data plotted in Figure 6 show turn-signal use for both stores during the period before and after the two paycheck inserts. A slight increase in turn-signal use was observed concurrent with policy onset. Mean turn-signal use at Store A was 70% over a seven-week baseline period, 78% during the two-week period between the first and second policy statement, and 84% during the four-week period after the second policy statement. Mean turn-signal use at Store B was 46% over a nine-week baseline period, 51% during the two-week period between the first and second policy statements, and 59% during the two-week period following the final policy intervention.

Further analysis of the data revealed that deliverers (n = 29) whose baseline turn-signal use was between 40% and 75% increased their use of turn signals an average of 16 percentage points. This is in contrast to those deliverers (n = 18) whose baseline turn-signal use was below 40%. These employees only averaged an increase of 2 percentage points. Pizza deliverers (n = 13) whose baseline turn-signal use was above 75% were not included in this analysis because an evaluation of their data was biased by a ceiling effect.

Implications

These data suggest that the safest drivers were the first to comply with the safe driving policy. Policy statements, such as state safety-belt laws or organizational safety edicts such as the one used in this study, often target a large number of people and are not usually intrusive to the individual unless enforced with consequences such as citations or dismissals. The MIL model predicts that these low-intrusive interventions will have difficulty influencing the most risky drivers. This is problematic according to Waller (1987b) who suggested "those segments of the driving population who are least likely to comply with safe driving laws are precisely those groups that are at highest risk of serious injury" (p. 43).

This presumed direct relationship between risky behavior and non-

FIGURE 6. Percent weekly turn-signal use across baseline and intervention (i.e., two administrations of a turn-signal policy statement) phases at Stores A and B during Ludwig and Geller (1999a). Vertical lines around data points represent the range of daily safety-belt use during that week.

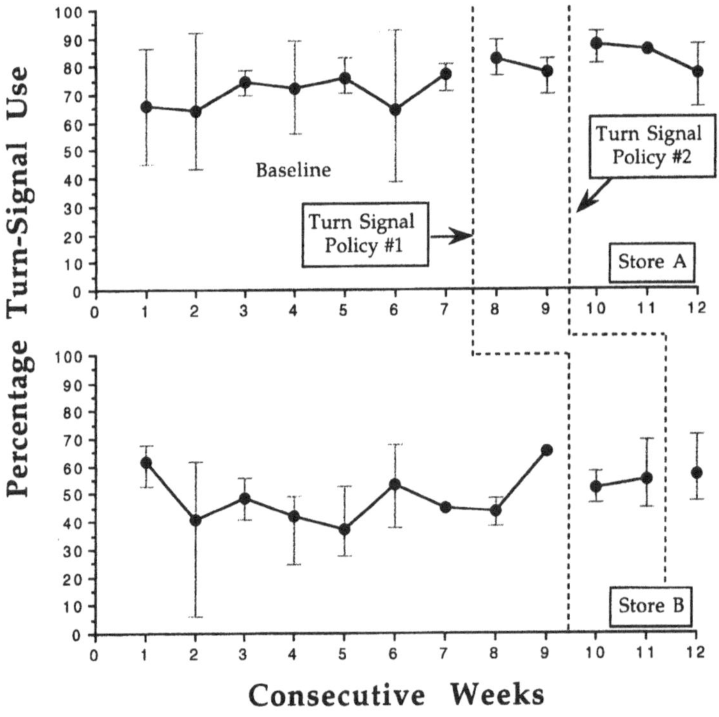

compliance with behavior change policy has other empirical support. Young males (Preusser, Williams, & Lund, 1985), persons with elevated blood alcohol (Wagenaar, 1984), and drivers with unsafe headway distances between their vehicles and the vehicle they are following (Evans, Wasielewski, & von Buseck, 1982) were found to be less likely to comply with driving policies. Thus, the most prominent decreases in injuries from vehicle crashes won't occur until the remaining individuals are impacted by other intervention strategies (Campbell et al., 1987). And, according to the MIL model, these need to be more intrusive and offer a higher agent-to-participant ratio (Geller et al., 1990).

Generalization Effects

The use of strong external consequences paired with a lack of employee involvement contributed to the lack of response generalization. Safety-belt use decreased during the period after the first policy statements. Mean safety-belt use at Store A was 78% during the baseline period, 65% during the period between policy statements, and 79% after the final policy statement. Mean safety-belt use at Store B was 74% during the baseline period, 59% during the period between policy statements, and 70% after the final policy statement. Data plotted in Figure 7 show safety-belt use for both stores before and after the turn-signal policies.

One possible explanation for this result is the behavioral phenomenon Skinner (1953, 1971) called countercontrol. Planned actions by some pizza deliverers may have been aimed at thwarting the agents' (i.e., managers and researchers) attempts to control their behavior. According to Skinner (1974) countercontrol behaviors are often directed at agencies and institutions such as organized religions, governments and economic systems that use their control over important reinforcers to create aversive contingencies that, in the long run, result in exploitation of those controlled.

> They escape from the controller–moving out of range if he is an individual, or defecting from a government, becoming an apostate from a religion, resigning, or playing truant–or they may attack in order to weaken or destroy the controlling power, as in a revolution, a reformation, a strike, or a student protest. In other words, *they oppose control with countercontrol.* (Skinner, 1974, p. 190, emphasis added)

Examples of countercontrol primarily demonstrate undesirable changes in behaviors targeted by the controlling intervention. In this study we did not see any notable examples of individuals exhibiting this type of countercontrol by decreasing their turn-signal use in response to the controlling intervention. However, we did see individuals and the group as a whole decrease their safety-belt use in response to the policy. This finding would suggest that researchers consider an

FIGURE 7. Percent weekly safety-belt use across baseline and intervention (i.e., two administrations of a turn-signal policy statement) phases at Stores A and B during Ludwig and Geller (1999a). Vertical lines around data points represent the range of daily safety-belt use during that week.

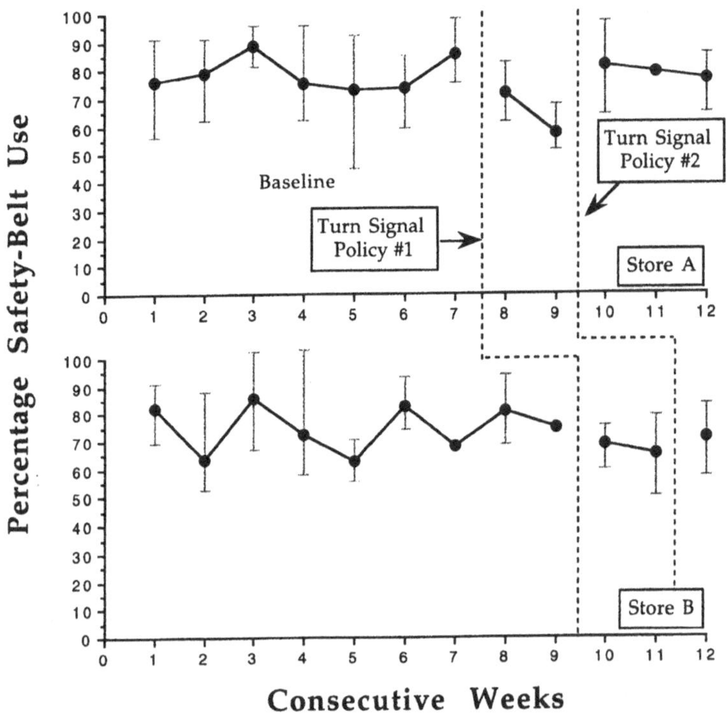

expanded definition of countercontrol to include undesirable changes in non-targeted behaviors.

The awareness and promise-card program in the first study (Ludwig & Geller, 1991) had a high level of employee involvement and appeared to influence response generalization or desirable changes in a non-targeted behavior. In contrast, the policy statement in Ludwig and Geller (1999a) had a high level of external control and solicited no employee involvement. Rather than response generalization, a non-targeted behavior decreased in frequency, suggesting the possibly of countercontrol. Our next study sought to test this distinction more directly by manipulating the level of involvement and external control.

ASSIGNED VERSUS PARTICIPATORY GOAL SETTING AND FEEDBACK (LUDWIG & GELLER, 1997)

In our investigation of employee involvement, we came across a debate in the goal-setting literature. Locke and Latham (1990) asserted that goal setting is a robust intervention in that it can improve all kinds of performance. They concluded that it didn't matter whether employees participated in goal setting or if goals were assigned solely by someone else. Meta-analyses by Mento, Steel, and Karren (1987) and Tubbs (1987) seemed to verify their claim. However, the studies reviewed by Locke and Latham (1990) only evaluated the impact of goal setting on the behavior(s) specified in the goal statement–the target behavior(s).

From our prior research, we hypothesized that a goal-setting intervention with a high level of involvement would lead to desirable response generalization. On the other hand, a goal-setting intervention with a low level of participation and a high level of managerial control might be accompanied by changes in non-targeted behaviors akin to countercontrol. To evaluate these hypotheses, we contrasted a goal-setting intervention that encouraged employee participation with one that did not.

Behaviors Observed

Turn-signal and safety-belt use were observed among drivers from three pizza delivery stores, along with our first attempt at observing intersection stopping. Baseline observations indicated that, of the three behaviors, complete intersection stopping was relatively infrequent and most in need of improvement. Safety-belt and turn-signal use were concurrently observed but not targeted by the intervention. Employees at one store participated in goal setting, and one week later, employees at the other store were assigned a goal. The third store served as a comparison store. A coin was flipped to assign conditions to stores.

Intervention

The employees at each treatment store attended an awareness meeting modeled after Ludwig and Geller (1991). However, the promise cards were replaced by the goal-setting procedure. Employees who participated in the goal setting were asked a series of questions about intersection stopping and discussed answers to these questions for roughly 45 minutes. Afterwards, the employees were asked if they believed that coming to a complete stop should be a policy of the store and if they could set a complete stopping goal for the group to attain. Everyone was encouraged to engage in the discussion that was followed by a vote on a specific percentage goal. Employees were then shown their current percentage of complete intersection stops on a graph that compared it with the goal they had set (indicated by a horizontal line starting at the Y-axis). Over the next four weeks this graph was used to display the weekly percentages of complete stops achieved by the entire group.

The participative group meeting was videotaped and the discussion was transcribed. The transcription was then developed into a lecture that was presented during an employee meeting at the second intervention store. This was done to assure the same information on complete stopping was delivered to both groups. It also provided verification that neither safety belts nor turn signals were mentioned at either meeting. Members of the Assigned Goal-Setting group were not given an opportunity to talk during the lecture. Instead of getting to set their goal, this group was assigned the same goal set by the participative group. They were then shown their current level of complete stops on a feedback graph that included a plot of the assigned goal.

From the videotapes, we calculated that employees in the Participative Goal Setting group spoke for a total of 14 minutes during their one-hour meeting, while employees in the Assigned group only spoke for a total of 5 seconds during their meeting that was just as long. Over the next four weeks, both groups received graphical feedback on their complete stops. Actually, the feedback the Participative and Assigned groups received was calculated from observations of both groups. Therefore, both groups received the same feedback.

Results

Data plotted in Figure 8 show the mean percentages of complete intersection stops over the course of this field study, summarized by weeks. Complete stops increased from a baseline of 54% to 66% during the intervention phase among pizza deliverers who received the participative goal-setting intervention. Among those who received the assigned goal-setting intervention, complete stopping increased from a baseline level of 45% to 69% during their intervention. After the intervention was withdrawn, frequency of complete stops among deliverers in both groups immediately trended downward and had returned to baseline levels when observed during follow-up. From withdrawal to follow-up, the mean percentage of complete intersection stopping decreased from 60% to 53% and from 59% to 42% for the Participative and Assigned groups, respectively.

Implications

Our results did not replicate the effects of participative and assigned goal-setting interventions in other published research studies. For example, a series of studies by Erez (Erez, 1986; Erez & Arad, 1986) found that participation in goal setting lead to superior performance. However, Locke and Latham (1990) argued that results such as these were not due to the amount of participation but rather to differences in mediating variables such as goal difficulty (Latham & Saari, 1979a; Latham, Steele, & Saari, 1982; Kernan & Lord, 1988), information (Latham & Saari, 1979b), experimental support (Latham, Erez, & Locke, 1988), and strategy development (Latham & Winters, 1989). Additionally, they cited studies where groups who participated in goal setting often set less specific and easier goals. After factoring in these variables, Locke and Latham (1990) found no appreciable differences in performance between assigned and participative goal setting.

Generalization Effects

With respect to response generalization, functional control of participative goal setting on each non-target behavior was evident. Data plotted in Figure 9 show the mean percentage of deliverers using their safety-belt per each week of this study. Pizza deliverers who received participative goal setting increased their safety-belt use from a base-

FIGURE 8. Percent weekly complete intersection stops across baseline, intervention, withdrawal, and follow-up phases from the participative, assigned, and control groups during Ludwig and Geller (1997). Vertical lines around data points represent the range of daily safety-belt use during that week.

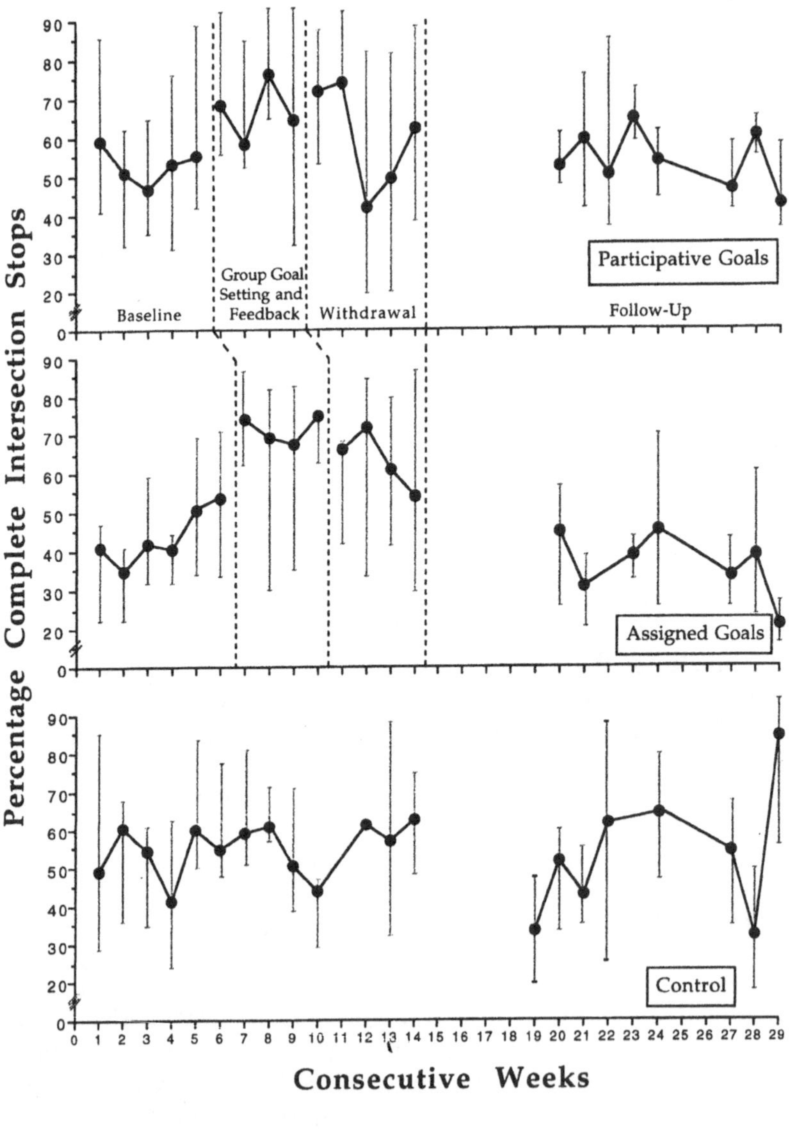

line of 75% to 85% during the complete stopping intervention. This increase continued into the withdrawal phase, eventually reaching 84% and was maintained at 88% during the longer-term follow-up phase.

Pizza deliverers who received assigned goal setting exhibited no change in mean safety-belt use from baseline to intervention. Their baseline and intervention mean safety-belt use rates were respectively 57% and 56% during the complete stopping intervention. Mean safety-belt use percentages were 58% and 61% during withdrawal and follow-up, respectively.

Data plotted in Figure 10 show the percentage of deliverers using turn-signals per consecutive weeks of this study. Pizza deliverers who received participative goal setting increased their turn-signal use from a baseline mean of 68% to 76% during the complete stopping intervention. This increase continued into the withdrawal phase to 78%, but declined during the longer-term follow-up phase to 72%. Pizza deliverers who were assigned their goal decreased their turn-signal use slightly, from a baseline mean of 66% to 62% during the intervention targeting complete stopping. Mean turn-signal use percentages were 53% and 51% during withdrawal and follow-up, respectively.

Implications

These results suggest the assigned intervention may have actually influenced undesired side effects in non-targeted behaviors. During assigned goal setting, the deliverers may have started coming to a complete stop at the main intersection because of the external contingencies provided by the mandated goal, feedback, and managerial surveillance. The deliverers in the Assigned group may have actively sought to avoid possible undesirable consequences of disobeying their manager.

It is reasonable to assume that, although not explicitly stated in the meeting, failure to comply with the manager's policy could result in such negative employment outcomes as unfavorable scheduling or even dismissal. In fact, some employees may have had experience, personal or vicarious, with these kinds of consequences in the past. Therefore, the higher increase in complete stops in the Assigned group may have been due to this potential establishing operation (Mawhinney & Fellows-Kubert, 1999). Interestingly, many deliverers in the Assigned group seemingly demonstrated reactivity to the overt control

FIGURE 9. Percent weekly safety-belt use across baseline, intervention, withdrawal, and follow-up phases from the participative, assigned, and control groups during Ludwig and Geller (1997). Vertical lines around data points represent the range of daily safety-belt use during that week.

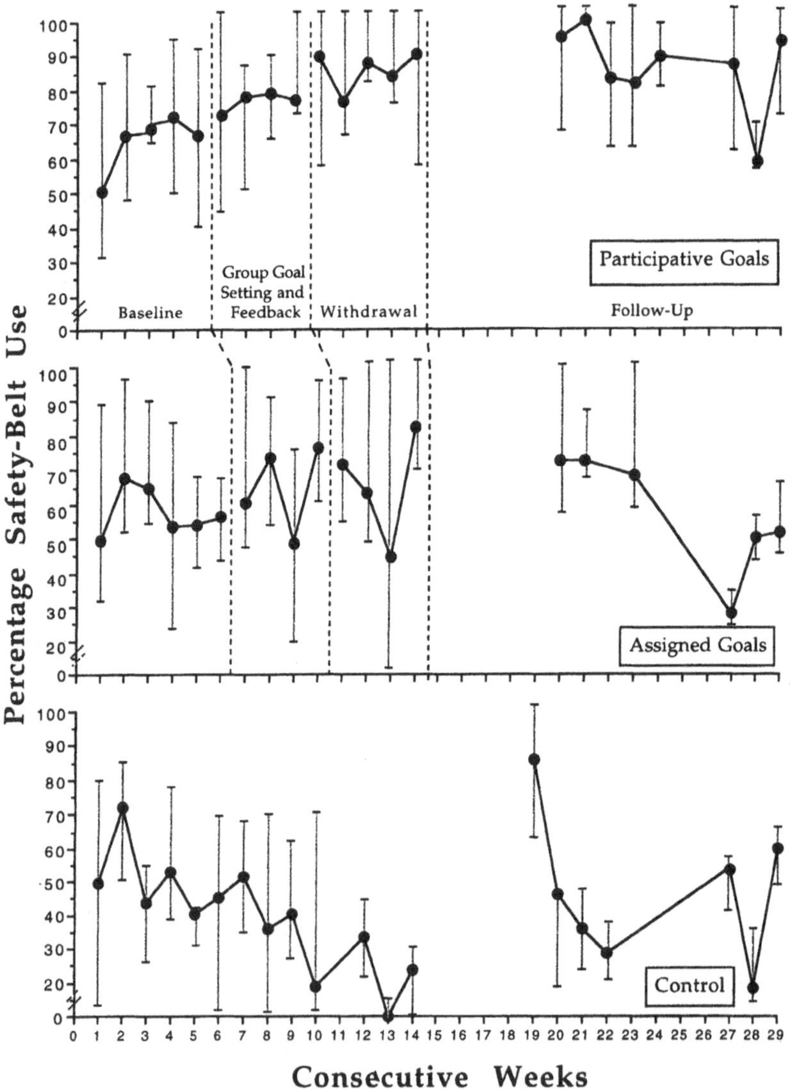

FIGURE 10. Percent weekly turn-signal use across baseline, intervention, withdrawal, and follow-up phases from the participative, assigned, and control groups during Ludwig and Geller (1997). Vertical lines around data points represent the range of daily safety-belt use during that week.

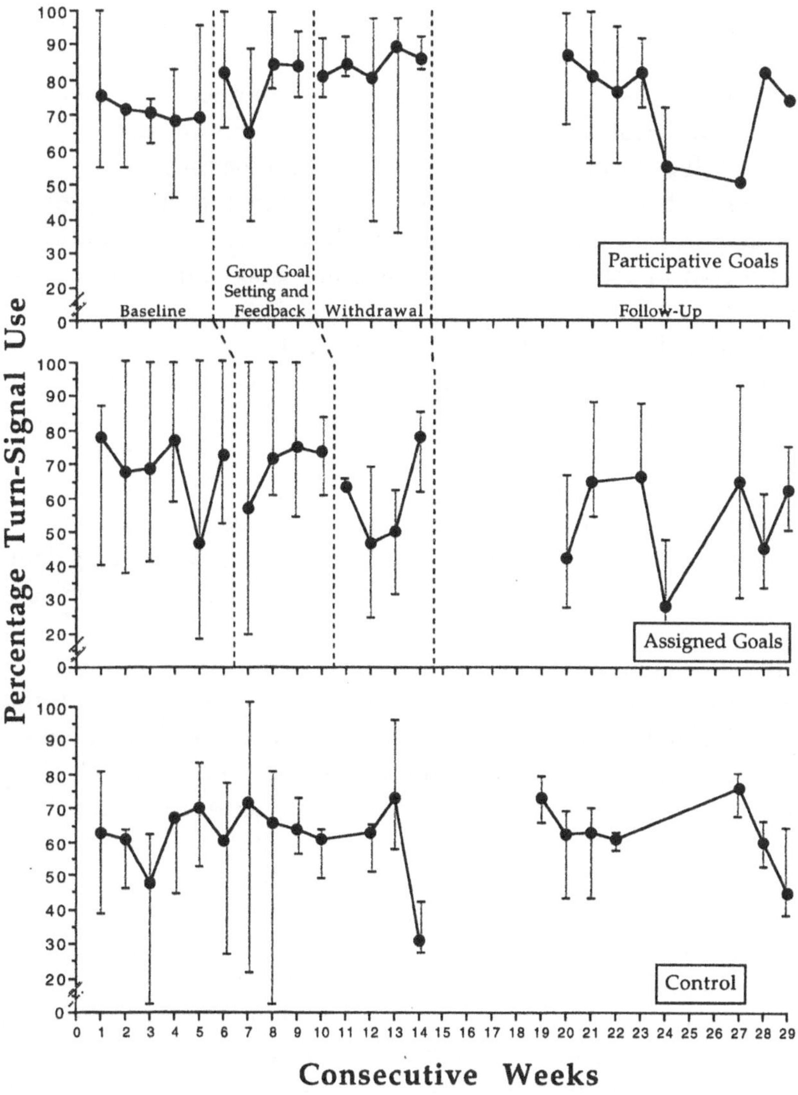

by decreasing related safe-driving behaviors not targeted by the manager's mandate.

Many companies fail to capitalize on beneficial side effects of their safety programs. They rely primarily on the practice of mandating policies and other controlling contingencies while failing to appreciate the positive results associated with involving employees in policy implementation. Fortunately, this fact has not been lost on U.S. policy makers. In a proposed safety and health program rule, the Occupational Safety and Health Administration (OSHA, 1999) requires employers to establish a workplace safety and health program to comply with standards set by OSHA. They specify in this rule that such a program must, as a "core element," provide employees with opportunities for participation in establishing, implementing, and evaluating the program.

Ludwig and Geller (1997) reported evidence that goal setting is a highly effective procedure for allowing drivers to participate in the interventions aimed at increasing their safe driving. We were able to compare participative versus assigned goal setting in a group context, thereby manipulating key involvement and external control variables from the Behavior Change Taxonomy. Thus, we were able to test tenets of the Behavior Change Taxonomy while also devising interventions that influenced whether a desirable or undesirable spread of effect occurred (i.e., response generalization or countercontrol).

Although aggregated group results were positive, Ludwig and Geller (1991, 1999a) presented data suggesting that not all participants exhibited desirable changes in safety behaviors in response to group-based interventions. Similarly, some employees' lack of change may be "hidden" within the presentation of group feedback. These unaffected individuals are likely the ones most in need of change and, within group goal setting, they can easily be ignored. The MIL model predicts that a more intrusive intervention is needed to change the behavior of individuals who may otherwise "fall through the cracks" of a group feedback technique. Our next study was designed to address the question concerning whether a more intrusive individual feedback technique could be used to "capture" some of the individuals initially unresponsive to a group feedback technique.

GROUP GOAL SETTING WITH PUBLIC INDIVIDUALIZED FEEDBACK (LUDWIG, GELLER, & CLARKE, 1999)

For this study, we initially established a group goal accompanied by group feedback in much the same manner as the participative group in the study described above (Ludwig & Geller, 1997). In the context of this group goal and feedback system, participants could not tell which of their coworkers were contributing to the group's accomplishments. Without public individualized feedback "social loafing" (Latane, Williams, & Hawkins, 1979) can be expected.

According to the Behavior Change Taxonomy, peer support is an important determinant of intervention effectiveness. Initially, we defined peer support loosely as interactions between individuals involved in the intervention. When we conducted the participative goal setting in the Ludwig and Geller (1997) study, however, we noticed that employees recognized each other orally for behaviors that contributed to attaining their group's goal. Additionally, it is possible individuals in the Participative group who were noticed performing behaviors inconsistent with the group goal were subjected to aversive treatment by other group members until they engaged in goal-supportive behavior.

Behaviors that imply peer support (e.g., prompting another driver's safe behavior, verbally praising a driver returning from a trip) and peer pressure (e.g., scolding a non-compliant peer) may contribute significantly to group goal attainment. Group members' methods of influencing each other's behavior, in this example, parallel the principles of positive and negative reinforcement. Incidentally, we did not notice these peer interactions in the Assigned Goal-Setting group. Instead, it was the manager who delivered praise and reprimands.

When feedback is aggregated at the group level, the process of determining which peers were contributing to a group goal and those who were not is inferential at best. If a group goal is agreed upon and then separate individual feedback is also publicly posted, peers can be in a better position to exert interpersonal influence. Ludwig, Geller, and Clarke (1999) studied this by providing public individualized feedback in the context of a group goal. In this situation, peer support should be facilitated because everyone in the group is aware of each other's contribution toward the group goal. We agree with Poling,

Smith, and Braatz (1993) who called for more systematic measures of these types of variables.

The MIL model provides an alternative way of conceptualizing the Ludwig, Geller, and Clarke (1999) study. The MIL model suggests that an intervention will be more effective when it is more intrusive. The word "intrusive" has a negative connotation because it suggests an invasion of privacy. Our use of the term implies that intervention operations could be tailored more precisely for the individual. One way of doing this is to provide information to individuals about their own behavior through individualized feedback.

Experimental Design

The design of this study was a multiple baseline across two stores with an additional comparison store. The time series design contained three phases in an ABCA format. Baseline observations of complete intersection stops, turn-signal use, and safety-belt use among pizza deliverers were conducted at the three stores. Analysis of the baseline data revealed that turn-signal use had the most stable baseline in the target pizza delivery locations. Therefore, turn-signal use was selected as the target behavior.

Because our intervention consisted of giving individuals direct feedback, we were concerned the drivers would wonder who was observing them to provide the feedback. In the Ludwig and Geller (1997) study we gave store managers hand-held counters and told the employees their group feedback came from that source. This was not acceptable when using individual feedback because the person's name (or other identifier) had to be recorded. Our solution was to put additional observers in the store to provide an ostensive source of feedback. From this vantage-point, we were also able to observe some of the peer support behaviors occurring in the store.

Comparison Groups. Another feature of this study is that we used four comparison groups in addition to the two treatment groups. History confounds (such as events occurring in the environment at the same time as the intervention) are common when intervening to improve driving safety. A comparison group of civilians was also observed in an attempt to control for the potential impact of driving safety messages provided by the national media and other events such as changes in laws that might influence the general population's driving during the intervention.

A pizza delivery store in the same town as the treatment stores was used as a comparison store in an attempt to "control" for changes due to local driving safety campaigns and other events that might have had an impact on pizza deliverers during our intervention. Finally, two additional stores in a different town were used as comparison stores. These stores were franchises of the same corporations as the treatment stores and were intended to serve as comparison stores in an effort to control for internal driving policy changes and safe driving promotions at the two corporations. For example, as a result of a report of our research results published in one corporation's *Pepperoni Press,* we previously had to abort an intervention project.

Intervention

After the baseline observation phase, the interventions began at staggered time intervals across the two experimental stores. The first phase of the intervention was implemented at Store A, and one week later it was initiated at Store B. The intervention began with an all-employee meeting modeled after the Ludwig and Geller (1997) study. The benefits of using turn-signals were discussed for 20 minutes and then the group's current turn-signal use was presented. After this, the group was asked to set a group goal for turn-signal use to be reached within 8 weeks. Deliverers were then introduced to the group feedback poster that included their current mean turn-signal percentage with the group goal of 80% represented by a straight line drawn across the graph. Every 4 days thereafter, the group turn-signal use percentage was calculated and posted in time series format on the store's group feedback graph.

After 4 weeks, the second phase of the intervention began and a new feedback poster was placed in the stores. In addition to providing group turn-signal percentages along with the group goal, the new poster depicted each deliverer's name and weekly percentage of turn-signal use. Individual names and mean percentages were graphed on a vertical line above and below the group mean for a given week. This allowed the deliverers to see their mean turn-signal use in relation to the group mean as well as every other deliverer's percentage. The original group goal also appeared on the graph. Group and individual feedback were graphed in this manner for 4 consecutive weeks. Then all store graphs were removed. After a hiatus of 5 1/2 weeks, data collection resumed during an 8-week follow-up phase.

Results

Data plotted in Figure 11 show the turn-signal use for the intervention stores over the course of this study. Store A had an extremely low turn-signal use during baseline. They then increased their turn-signal use from a baseline mean of 6% to 21% during the group feedback phase. This usage increased to 32% when individual feedback was provided. Mean turn-signal use returned to a mean of 21% during the follow-up phase.

Deliverers at Store B also increased their turn-signal use from a baseline mean of 33% to 53% during the group feedback phase. An additional increase to a mean of 59% turn-signal use occurred when individual feedback was added. Mean turn-signal use returned to 36% during the follow-up phase at Store B. There were no significant changes in the same town comparison store (i.e., Store C), either of the same-corporation comparison stores (i.e., Stores D & E), or in the civilian sample concurrent with the two-phase intervention at the intervention stores (i.e., Stores A & B).

The impact of the group goal and feedback intervention on turn-signal use replicated the findings of Ludwig and Geller (1997) where the target behavior was intersection stopping. Both stores increased substantially over baseline following the group goal-setting and feedback intervention. In fact, the mean of the first intervention phase was higher than the top of the range of daily turn-signal use during baseline. Additional increases in mean percentages of turn-signal use occurred when individual percentages were added to the feedback graphs. This confirmed our hypothesis and prediction from the MIL model that individual feedback would provide additional impact beyond that produced by a group goal-setting and feedback intervention.

When we analyzed data from individual pizza deliverers who experienced the interventions at the two stores, we found an instructive distinction between those more versus less responsive to the interventions. Data plotted in Figure 12 show the data of 12 deliverers that increased their turn-signal use at least 15 percentage points over baseline after the group goal-setting and feedback intervention. These deliverers are contrasted with 10 pizza deliverers who did not show a

FIGURE 11. Percent weekly turn-signal use across baseline, group goal-setting and feedback intervention, public individualized feedback intervention, and follow-up phases at Stores A, B, C, D, E, and civilian control during Ludwig, Geller, and Clarke (1999).

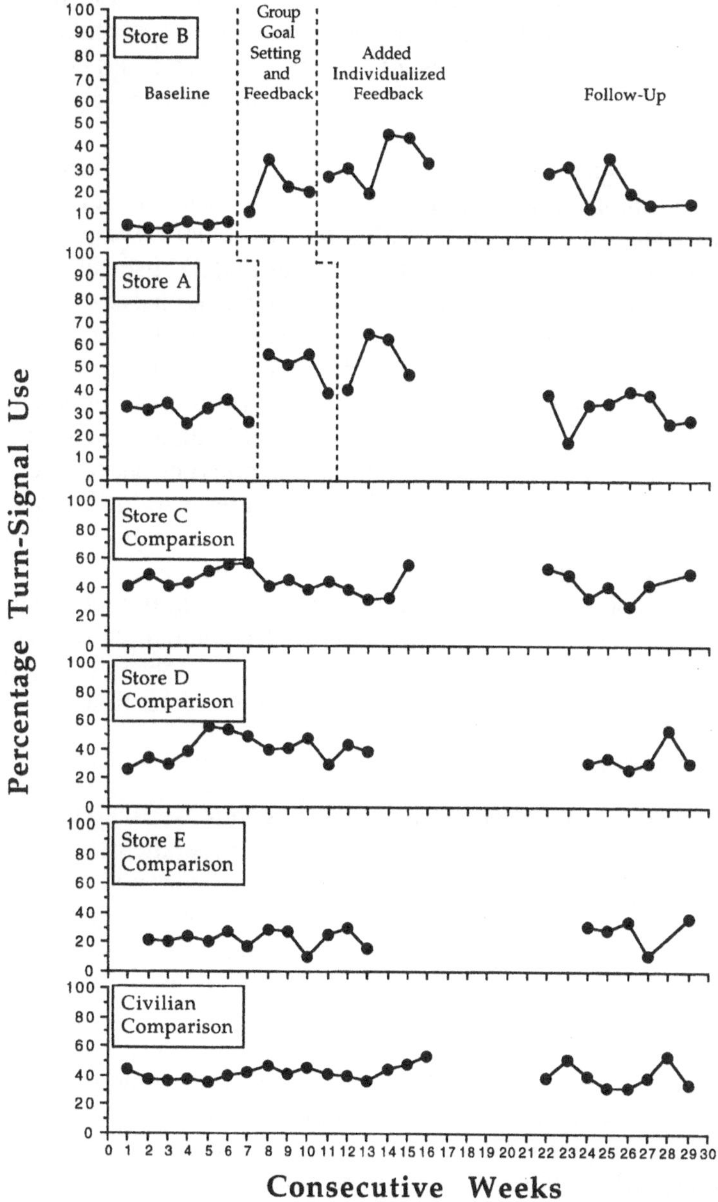

15 percentage-point increase over baseline during the group goal-setting and feedback intervention.

The initial increase of aggregated group turn-signal use (shown in Figure 11) that occurred during the group goal setting and feedback came primarily from the 12 deliverers with over 15 percentage point increases over baseline. The rest of the pizza deliverers did not change as a result of the group-based intervention. During the publicly posted individualized feedback, most of the 12 pizza deliverers who increased turn-signal use during the group-based intervention did not continue to improve when individualized feedback was added. However, the group of 10 pizza deliverers who were not responsive to the group-based intervention increased their turn-signal use substantially during the publicly posted individualized feedback phase.

Taken together, the patterns of group and individual behavior across baselines and interventions lend credence to predictions of the MIL model regarding relative effectiveness of various intervention techniques and combinations of them. Those individuals who increased their turn-signal use during the group-based intervention, for the most part, did not benefit from a more intrusive intervention. In contrast, those pizza deliverers who did not change their turn-signal use during the first intervention did increase their turn-signal use when they subsequently encountered a more intrusive intervention. In fact, when we posted these individuals' percentages in the context of their more successful peers, rather dramatic increases were observed in their turn-signal use. More intrusiveness led to more intervention impact.

Generalization Effects

There were no overall differences in safety-belt use as a result of the turn-signal intervention. Absence of response generalization between these two behaviors was unexpected because we had found a spread of effect from safety-belt use to turn-signal use in two previous studies (Ludwig & Geller, 1991, 1999b). We anticipated a reciprocal relationship whereby an intervention targeting turn-signal use would generalize to safety-belt use.

Analysis of the chain of behaviors that occur when a vehicle is entered and operated might shed some light on the non-reciprocal relationship between a driver's use of a safety belt and turn signal. Our observations of pizza deliverers suggest that most people who use their safety belt buckle up in the first moments of entering their ve-

FIGURE 12. Average percentage turn-signal use across baseline, group goal-setting and feedback intervention, public individualized feedback intervention, and follow-up phases during Ludwig, Geller, and Clarke (1999). The filled squares represent deliverers who increased their use of turn signals at least 15 percentage points during the group goal-setting and feedback intervention. The open circles represent deliverers who did not increase their use of turn signals at least 15 percentage points during the group goal-setting and feedback intervention.

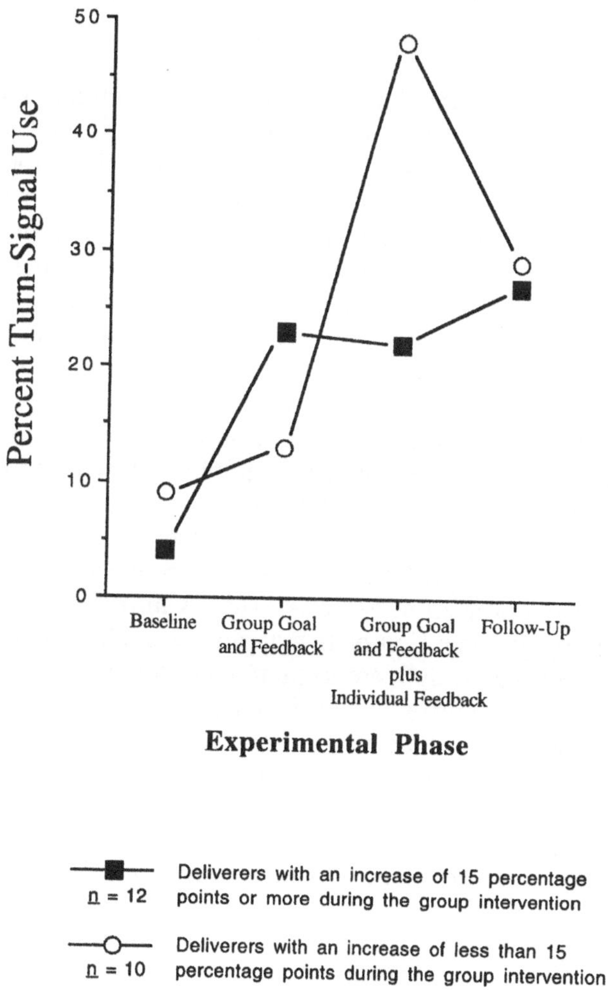

hicles, usually before reaching their first intersection. Therefore, safety-belt use usually precedes turn-signal use. Drivers who increase their use of a safety-belt during an intervention will be using their safety-belt when the opportunity to use a turn-signal occurs (i.e., at an intersection). The reverse does not typically occur. Drivers who increase their turn-signal use as a result of an intervention generally are not using their turn-signal when they first put on their safety-belt. Thus, the direction of this response chain may explain our finding of generalization from safety-belt to turn-signal use, not from turn-signal to safety-belt use.

In this study, there was a notable increase in complete intersection stops during the interventions that targeted turn-signal use. Data plotted in Figure 13 show the complete intersection stops for the experimental stores over the course of this study. Deliverers at Store A increased their complete intersection stops moderately from a baseline mean of 12% to 16% during the group feedback phase. Then complete intersection stops increased moderately to a mean of 18% during the publicly posted individualized feedback phase. Subsequently, complete intersection stops continued to increase during follow-up to 21%.

Deliverers at Store B also increased their complete intersection stops modestly from a baseline mean of 30% to 35% during the group feedback phase, then to 48% when the publicly posted individualized feedback was added. During follow-up, however, mean complete intersection stops decreased to 36%. The substantial increase in complete stops during the public individualized feedback phase observed at Store B was not seen at Store A. This is most likely because of intersection topography. Complete stopping was not as much a necessity at Store B because deliverers entered a two-lane road instead of a four-lane road. There were no significant variations in complete intersection stops among deliverers at the comparison stores or among the observations of civilians made concurrent with the two-phase intervention at the intervention stores.

Response generalization between turn-signal use and complete stopping can again be explained by considering the chain of behaviors occurring while driving. Use of a turn-signal and depressing vehicle brakes to stop at an intersection occur almost simultaneously. Therefore it is likely drivers who use their turn-signals in response to an intervention will often do so as they begin to apply brakes while approaching an intersection. In this case, generalization would be

FIGURE 13. Percent weekly complete intersection stops across baseline, group goal-setting and feedback intervention, public individualized feedback intervention, and follow-up phases at Stores A, B, C, D, E, and civilian control during Ludwig, Geller, and Clarke (1999).

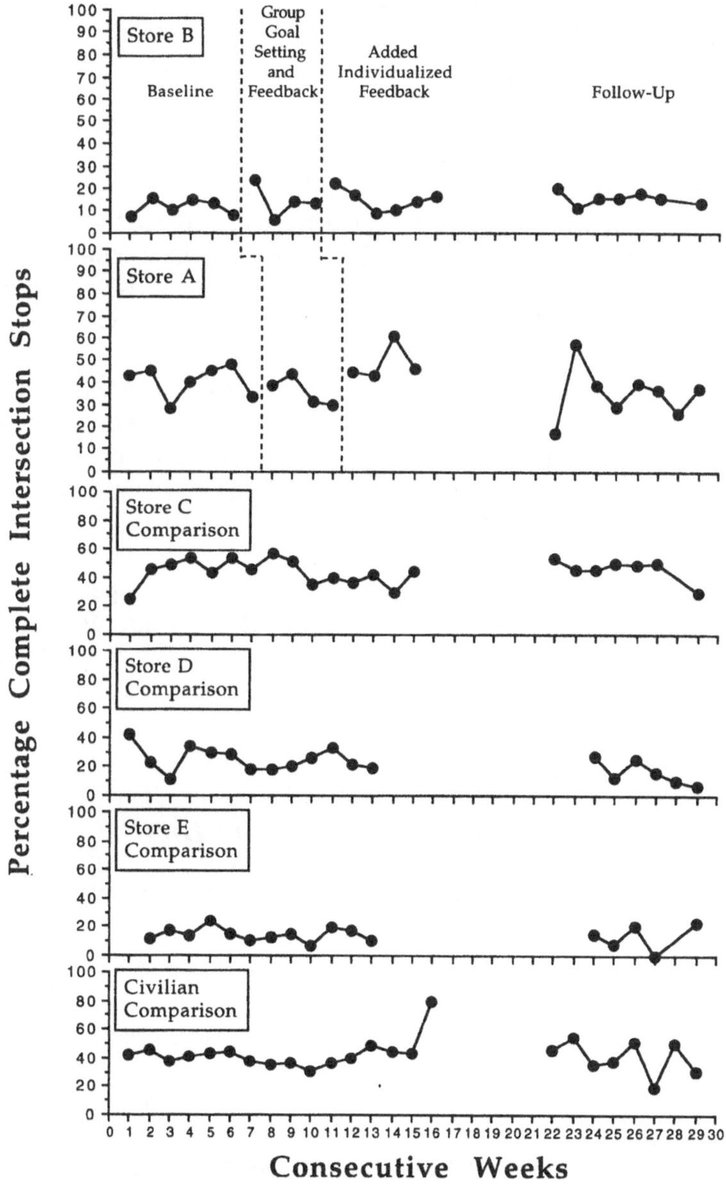

expected to occur in both directions, and such reciprocity was supported by our research. In addition to this study, Ludwig and Geller (1997) found a significant increase in turn-signal use during a participative intervention that targeted complete stopping at intersections.

It is noteworthy that the greatest response generalization occurred during the publicly posted individualized feedback phase. During this phase, we actually expected the most differentiation of the target behavior by the intervention and less susceptibility to generalization, at least to the extent this mechanism is related to induction (Catania, 1979). Induction had been described in the literature as a phenomenon that occurs when the operant is not differentiated by the reinforcer. However, it seems as though the public individualized feedback intervention should have further differentiated turn-signal use as the target of the intervention, yet complete stopping at Store B increased dramatically during this procedure.

The presentation of public individualized feedback in the context of a common goal may have been conducive to peer support. Instead of creating an environment of mutual support based on a common goal, the next study exposed participants to competitive reward contingencies. We anticipated that individuals working under these contingencies would give minimal peer support. Rather, the opposite would be more likely. Competition may create a context where peers actively avoid prompting and reinforcing the target behavior among their peers. The next study attempted to evaluate this kind of intervention by replacing a group goal with individual rewards for those who emitted the target behavior most often.

PUBLIC INDIVIDUALIZED FEEDBACK WITH COMPETITION (LUDWIG, BIGGS, WAGNER, & GELLER, 1999)

A number of studies in the safety literature have shown beneficial effects of individualized feedback techniques in the absence of goal setting. For example, when police received individual behavioral feedback from in-vehicle tachograph recorders vehicle crashes were reduced (Larson, Schnelle, Kirchner, Carr, Domash, & Risley, 1980). Also, Alavosius and Sulzer-Azaroff (1986) used individual feedback to improve the lifting and transferring of disabled clients among human service providers. Similar individual feedback techniques improved safety behaviors in a coal mine (Rhoton, 1980).

Individual rewards provide feedback that a certain behavior is desirable, and have been quite effective at increasing safe driving behaviors. Most of these programs have involved the direct and immediate delivery of small prizes to vehicle occupants observed using their safety belts (see review by Geller, 1984). Most of these interventions targeted adults in vehicles at entrances/exits to industrial complexes (e.g., Geller, 1983; Stutts, Hunter, & Campbell, 1984), at the exchange windows of banks (Geller, Johnson, & Pelton, 1982), and at the entrances to the parking lots of high schools (Campbell, Hunter, & Stutts, 1984), a university (Geller, Paterson, & Talbott, 1982), and a shopping mall (Elman & Killebrew, 1978). Also, Roberts and his colleagues successfully applied immediate reward strategies to increase children's use of child safety seats and safety belts (e.g., Roberts & Fanurick, 1986; Roberts & Turner, 1986; Roberts & Layfield, 1987). Whether targeting adults or children, when reward programs were withdrawn, in virtually all such instances mentioned above, the use of safety-belts declined, but usually remained above pre-intervention baseline levels.

A few accounts of the use of competition in organizational behavior management are relevant here. Kortick and O'Brien (1996) divided employees at a package delivery company into 14 teams who were given points based on quality control measures. These teams competed, had playoffs, and finally a "world series" to determine the winner of tangible rewards. This team competition was associated with increases in quality measures. In contrast, Ferguson and Blampied (1991) found that competition for rewards in conjunction with performance feedback produced no increases in the use of bicycle lights among individual bikers in New Zealand. Finally, Allison, Silverstein, and Galante (1992) found teacher assistants performed better in a cooperative condition than in a competitive condition.

Method

Pizza deliverers at five pizza stores (the same two intervention and three comparison sites used in the previous study) were observed for 5 weeks of baseline observations. Intersection stopping was the lowest and most stable during baseline among deliverers at Store A. Turn-signal use was the lowest and most stable during baseline among deliverers at Store B. Therefore, complete stopping was the target behavior for Store A, and turn-signal use was selected as the target behavior for Store B.

Intervention

This study used competitive rewards such that the pizza deliverer who performed the target behavior most often received an award while others received no award. The onset of the intervention was staggered between Store A and Store B by one week. Obtrusive in-store observations began two weeks before the intervention. Each deliverer's target behavior was calculated and graphed weekly for five weeks on a feedback poster similar to that used by Ludwig, Geller, and Clarke (1999).

Contest rules, displayed at each store, explained that weekly target behavior averages for each deliverer would be posted and the deliverer with the highest percentage of the target behavior each week would be awarded a prize. The weekly winners choose from an assortment of automobile-related prizes, including free oil changes, car washes, and tire rotations. In addition to weekly winners, the deliverer with the highest cumulative targeted behavior at the end of the contest would be awarded a "grand prize."

Roughly 3 months prior to the intervention, we asked pizza deliverers what type of reward they would find valuable (other than money). Geller (1998a) proposed that choosing incentives prior to treatment increases the reinforcing value of a reward and therefore supports higher safety performance. The deliverers mentioned that rewards could be used to keep their cars in good repair. As a result, we solicited local business to donate a car maintenance product or service worth roughly $20. We obtained free car washes, oil changes, tire rotations, and products from auto parts stores. In exchange for a donation, businesses were mentioned on safety advertisements glued to outgoing pizza box tops. However, distribution of these box top advertisements did not occur until the data collection for the entire experiment was concluded.

Results

As the data plotted in Figure 14 show, deliverers at Store A increased their turn-signal use immediately, from a baseline mean of

35% to a mean of 58% (a 61% increase over baseline) as a result of the public individualized feedback and competition intervention targeting turn-signal use. During the withdrawal phase, mean turn-signal use among deliverers at Store A decreased to a mean of 53%, but remained substantially above baseline.

As data plotted in Figure 15 show, deliverers at Store B increased their complete intersection stopping from a mean of 14% during baseline to an intervention mean of 31% (a 117% increase above baseline). Then during withdrawal, mean complete intersection stopping decreased to 21%, a level 48% above baseline. Even though targeted by the intervention at Store B, complete intersection stops at this store did not increase immediately at the beginning of the public individualized feedback-competition intervention.

An appreciable increase in complete intersection stops was not evident until sometime into the third week of the intervention. Complete intersection stopping then exhibited an upward spike 50 percentage points above baseline and eventually declined to baseline levels near the end of the intervention period. It remained at the baseline level throughout the withdrawal phase.

This was the first time we compared intervention impact on two different driving behaviors. Store A's deliverers increased their turn-signal use quicker and more substantially than did Store B's deliverers with their target behavior (i.e., complete stops). This may have been due to the differing topographies of the two behaviors, nominal or implicit response costs associated with each, or histories with other interventions (e.g., driver training) that had targeted these behaviors. Additionally, these results may have been due to different work contexts (e.g., establishing operations) within the two stores or adjacent driving environments. For this reason the geography and road conditions of each store are relevant. It is probable that the four-lane road adjacent to Store B with excellent visibility in each direction limited the degree to which deliverers came to a complete stop, from baseline through intervention.

Winners vs. Non-Winners. The different patterns of responding to the intervention could have also been due to the distribution of winners at each store. At Store A, the rewards were won by many different deliverers; whereas at Store B, one particular deliverer was a consistent winner.

Data plotted in Figure 16 show the turn-signal use among deliverers

FIGURE 14. Percent weekly turn-signal use across baseline, public individualized feedback and competition intervention, and withdrawal phases at Stores A, B, C, D, E, and civilian comparison during Ludwig, Biggs, Wagner, and Geller (1999).

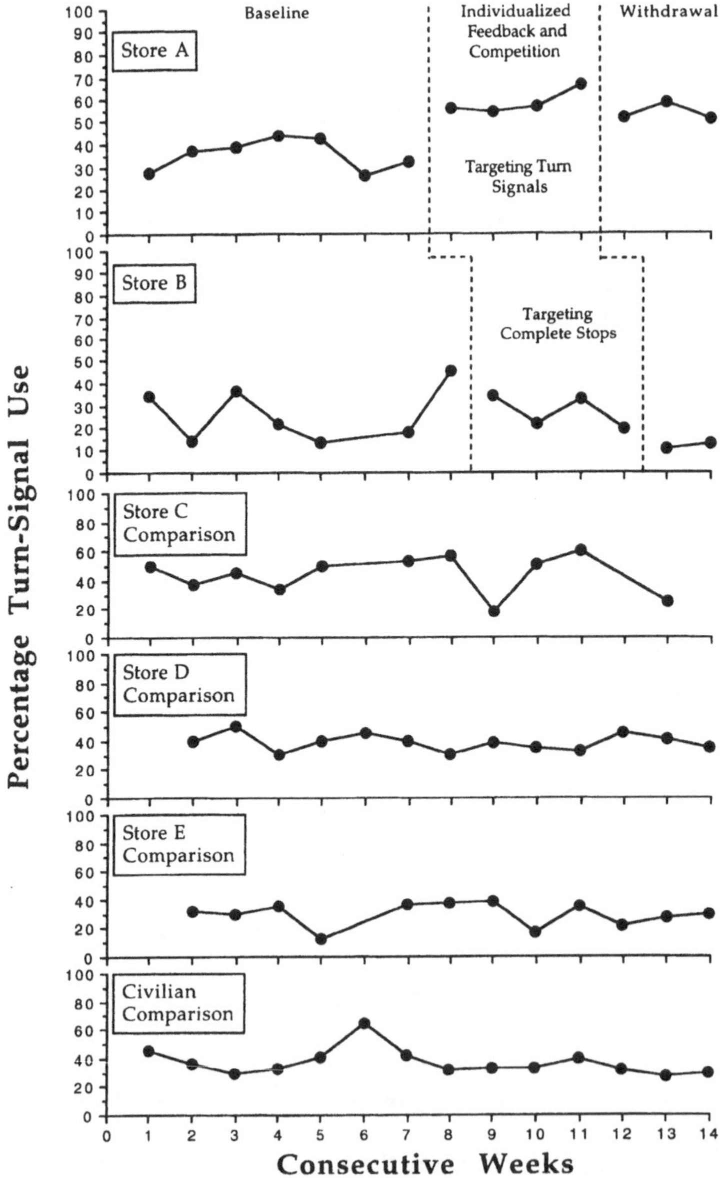

FIGURE 15. Percent weekly complete intersection stops across baseline, public individualized feedback and competition intervention, and withdrawal phases at Stores A, B, C, D, E, and civilian comparison during Ludwig, Biggs, Wagner, and Geller (1999).

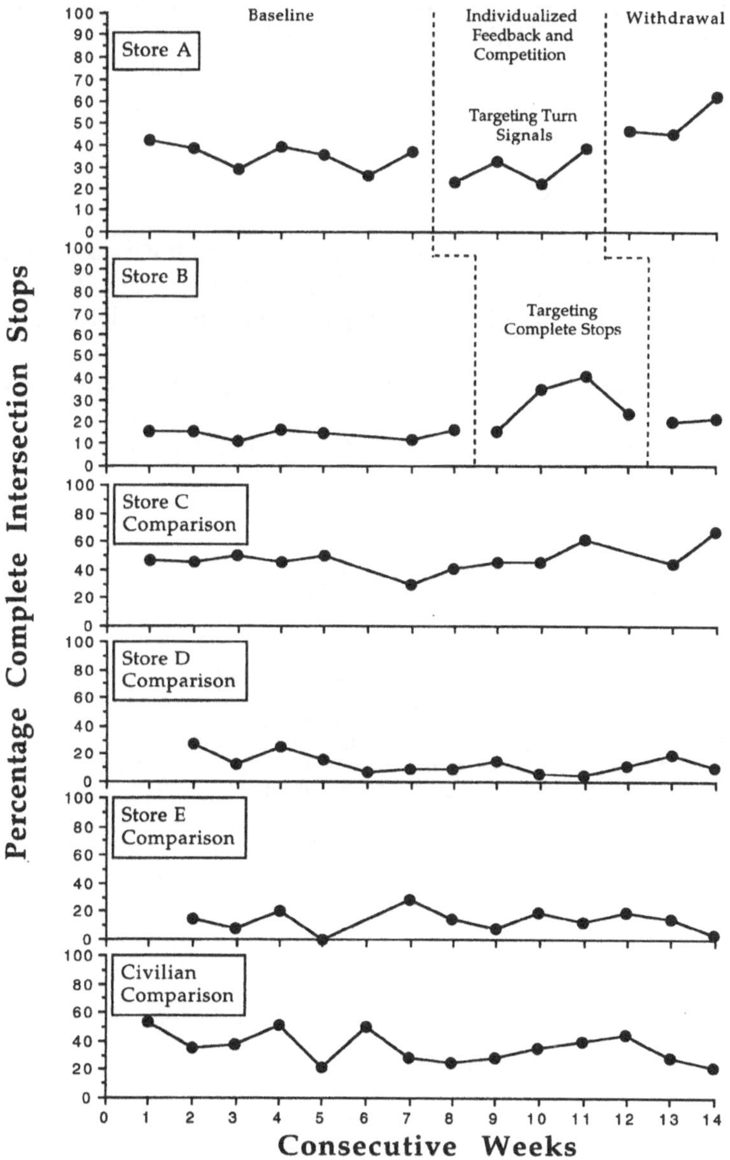

at Store A and the complete stopping among deliverers at Store B, divided between reward winners and non-winners. Those who won one or more rewards had greater increases in turn-signal use or complete stops than those who did not win. However, the majority of people who never received a reward still had a substantial increase in the targeted behaviors. This is an important finding in that it demonstrates that under some circumstances winning need not be required in order for performance to be increased during competition for limited rewards.

Generalization Effects

With respect to response generalization, safety-belt use, depicted in Figure 17, did not increase among deliverers during Store A's intervention. However, safety-belt use did increase among deliverers at

FIGURE 16. Percent weekly turn-signal use (Store A) and complete intersection stops (Store B) across baseline, public individualized feedback and competition intervention, and withdrawal phases for winners and non-winners during Ludwig, Biggs, Wagner, and Geller (1999).

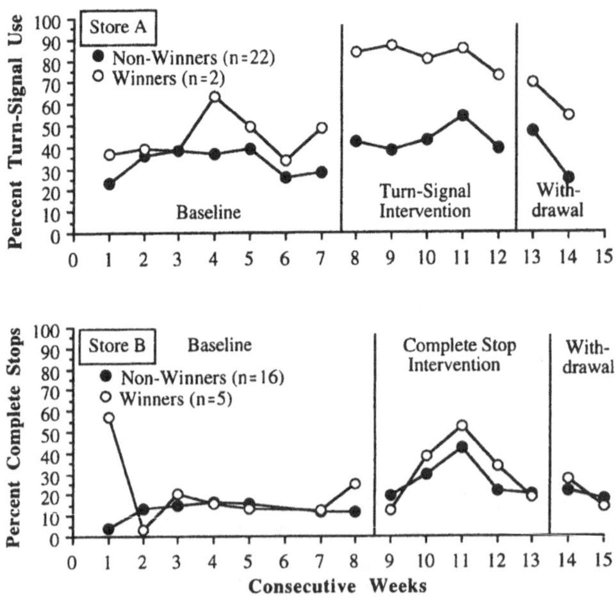

FIGURE 17. Percent weekly safety-belt use across baseline, public individualized feedback and competition intervention, and withdrawal phases at Stores A, B, C, D, E, and civilian comparison during Ludwig, Biggs, Wagner, and Geller (1999).

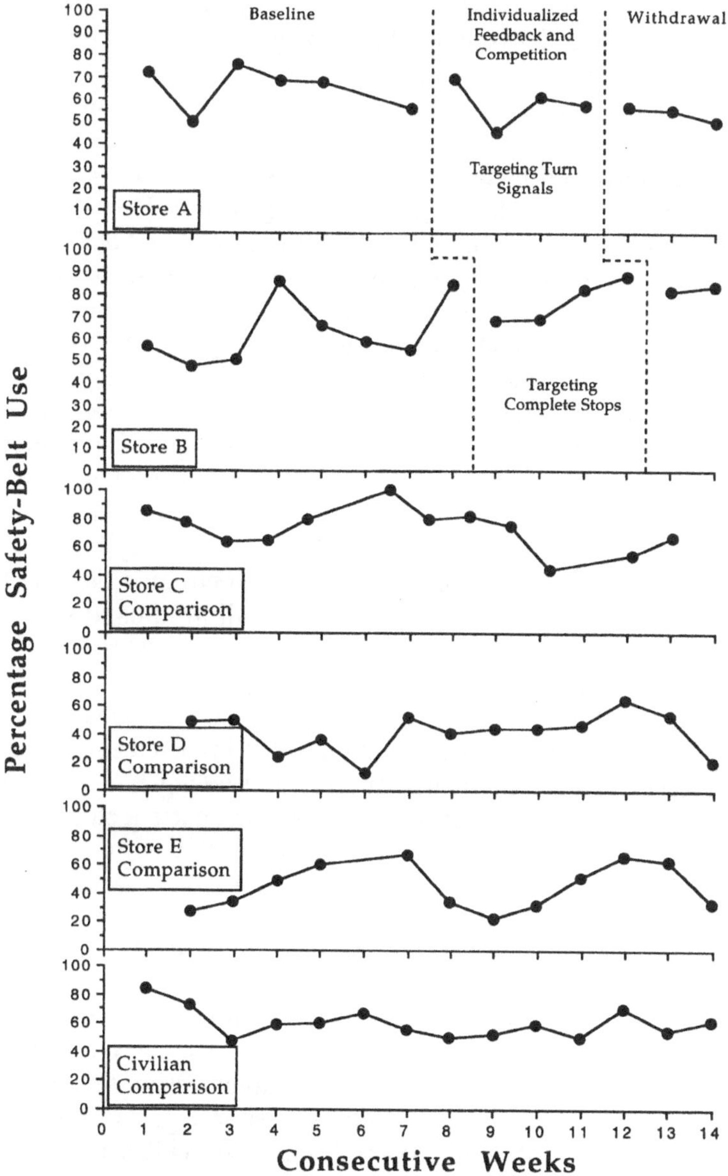

Store B, from a baseline mean of 59% to an intervention mean of 73%. And, mean safety-belt use during withdrawal increased even further to a mean of 86%. There were no changes in turn-signal use concurrent with the complete stopping intervention among deliverers at Store B. However, at the end of the intervention, turn-signal use decreased substantially among deliverers at Store B (where the intervention targeted complete intersection stopping), from means of 25% and 29% during baseline and intervention respectively, to 12% during withdrawal.

Complete intersection stopping at Store A did not seem to change during the intervention that targeted turn-signal use. However, when we made comparisons based on the direction turned or whether traffic was present (see Figure 18), we discovered a decrease in complete stopping among deliverers at Store A. Specifically, we found appreciable decreases in complete intersection stopping during the turn-signal intervention when the deliverers at Store A were turning left while traffic was present. This was somewhat disconcerting because the most dangerous turn to make is a left turn that requires a vehicle to cross lanes of oncoming traffic. This decrease in complete stopping was masked when looking at the overall data because complete stopping during right turns and during low traffic was already low and did not fall further because of a "floor" effect. Categorizing the data into different traffic and turn direction conditions allowed us to study the possible occurrence of countercontrol, an undesirable result of the intervention, that may have been otherwise overlooked.

Consistent with the Behavior Change Taxonomy, response generalization has been most prominent in studies that involved employees in intervention design and implementation (e.g., Ludwig & Geller, 1991, 1997, 1999b). Some of the pizza deliverers in the current study helped identify rewards for the competition, and weekly winners got to choose their reward. Otherwise, the intervention operations did not include much involvement. In fact, it could be argued that external consequences were prominent with minimal individual involvement. For example, the manager reviewed the public individualized feedback weekly and handed the winner the reward coupon in front of his/her peers. Such controlling operations may have caused the driver to differentiate between target and non-target responses (Catana, 1979) to a greater degree, thereby limiting response generalization.

Potential evidence of countercontrol was also evident in complete

FIGURE 18. Percent complete intersection stops across baseline, public individualized feedback and competition intervention, and withdrawal phases while traffic was present or not-present at Stores A and B during Ludwig, Biggs, Wagner, and Geller (1999).

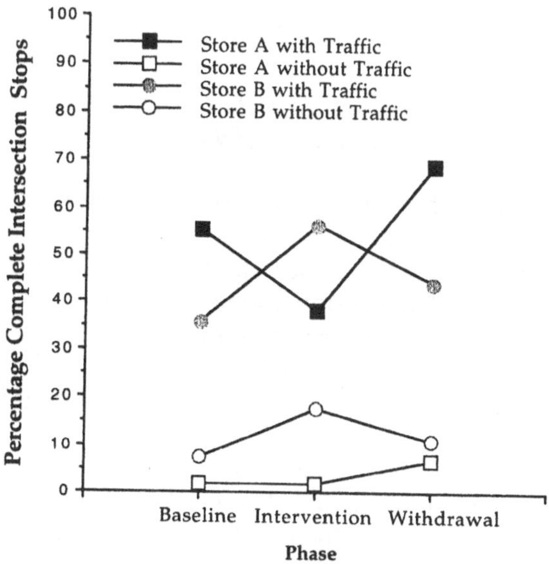

intersection stopping among deliverers at Store A. This evidence of countercontrol in response to controlling intervention operations is consistent with the Behavior Change Taxonomy and our previous studies using policies (Ludwig & Geller, 1999a) and assigned goal setting (Ludwig & Geller, 1997). These data also provide an interesting contrast to the Ludwig, Clarke, and Geller (1999) study, where there was ample evidence of response generalization and no instances of countercontrol even though public individualized feedback was used in both studies.

In the next study we provided pizza deliverers with individual goals and feedback. However, the goal setting and individual feedback were not public events. Instead, the goals were assigned and feedback given through private memos (a procedure used by Emmert, 1978). When the feedback is given privately, individuals' behavior cannot be subjected to examination by peers or managers. Additionally, when goals are assigned to individuals instead of groups, behavior is a function of only the reinforcement contingencies defined by the goal-setting event and subsequent feedback to the individual. Peer support should be low under these conditions because members of the pizza stores do not share a common and mutually-shared goal. The assignment of individualized goals also reduces involvement and implies external control.

STATIC VERSUS DYNAMIC GOAL SETTING (LUDWIG, 1999)

According to the behavior change taxonomy, individualized goals and feedback contribute a large amount of response information. Goals stipulate the specific behavior(s), the amount of desired behavior(s) requested, and often, the time frame for attaining the goal. All of our goal-setting interventions discussed thus far have used one final or ultimate goal that was static (i.e., did not change) and had a multi-week time frame (e.g., "80% *target behavior* within the next 4 weeks").

After being introduced, these static goals become only a reminder with no new response information. Feedback, on the other hand, not only stipulates the specific behavior(s), it also provides information about the current level of behavior. When feedback is regularly updated it provides new response information, especially if personalized. Likewise, goals that are made more *dynamic* (i.e., changing often) and focus on short-term achievement would periodically provide new response information as well.

If goals were presented in this same dynamic format and changed frequently based on individual performance, they would provide continual response information. In this case, goals would be combined with feedback to help direct behavior. This study manipulated whether private individualized goals remained static as an ultimate endpoint or were dynamic and changed as a function of individual performance. Because of greater response information for dynamic than static goals, the Behavior Change Taxonomy predicts that dynamic goals will have a greater impact on the target behavior than the static goals used most often in goal-setting studies, including our own studies.

Earlier treatment of the distinction between dynamic (or incremental) and static (or ultimate) goals focused on temporal differences between them. Bandura and Simon (1977) used the terms "proximal" and "distal" goals to define this temporal distinction. Proximity refers to the amount of time between two events (Kirschenbaum, 1985). A proximal goal provides for only a short amount of time between the establishment of a goal and its expected achievement. Alternatively, a distal goal involves a relatively larger amount of time between setting the goal and eventually achieving it.

The literature is not consistent regarding the effectiveness of distal versus proximal goal setting. Some studies present data suggesting that distal goal setting is more effective (Kirschenbaum, Humphrey, & Malett, 1981; Kirschenbaum, Malett, Humphrey, & Tomarken, 1982). Other research suggests that proximal goal setting is more effective (Bandura & Schunk, 1981; Cervone, 1989; Cervone & Peake, 1986; Hall, et al., 1987, Mischel & Patterson, 1976; Morgan, 1985). Nevertheless, the results of other studies suggest that these goal-setting approaches are equally effective (Bandura & Simon, 1977; Dubbert & Wilson, 1984; Fredda & Ludwig, 1999; Weinberg, Bruya, & Jackson, 1985). And many researchers have recommended the combination of both proximal and distal goals to achieve a desired level of performance (Bandura & Simon, 1977; Hall & Byrne, 1988). However, this proposal has not been tested.

These inconsistent conclusions suggest a temporal distinction does not adequately define this technique of setting one final goal versus setting a series of successively more challenging goals. Dynamic goals are usually more proximal and allow for goals to be adjusted many times. Static goals tend to be one-time events and are more distal. Additionally, static goals are more challenging (i.e., higher levels of performance required) than individual dynamic goals, because dynamic goals usually start small and build, eventually reaching the level of the static goal. The present study compared the effectiveness of three goal-setting techniques paired with private individualized feedback on safe driving behavior: (a) dynamic-only, (b) static-only, and (c) proximal plus static (i.e., proximal goals building to a static goal).

Method

In addition to two comparison groups, deliverers from three different pizza restaurants were given weekly private memos specifying a behavioral goal and offering individualized feedback. Because none of the intervention operations were public, we were able to randomly assign deliverers to the different goal-setting and feedback conditions.

Another benefit of this protocol was that we had an equal number of representatives from each store in the goal-setting groups. In addition, we attempted to make the baseline percentage of the target behavior (i.e., turn-signal use) equal across groups. The use of this stratified random assignment allowed us an amount of control over selection variables rarely achieved in field studies.

Baseline data were collected for six weeks. Then turn-signal use was chosen as the target behavior because it was the most stable and had the lowest frequency of occurrence. Observers were stationed both inside and outside each pizza store just like our other studies which included individualized feedback as an intervention technique (Ludwig, Geller, & Clark, 1999; Ludwig, Biggs, Wagner, & Clarke, 1999).

Intervention

The intervention ran for five weeks and was then followed by a six-week withdrawal phase. Each deliverer was given weekly individualized feedback in the form of a private memo that indicated the percentage of time that week the driver had used his/her turn-signal. Each memo also included a goal statement that varied according to the experimental condition assigned. Deliverers in the static condition were assigned one goal (i.e., a final goal of 80% turn-signal use) to be accomplished in 5 weeks. This goal was restated each week.

Deliverers in the dynamic condition were assigned new goals each week according to an incremental increase from individual baseline levels of turn-signal use. The incremental increase for the weekly dynamic goals were calculated by subtracting the individual's baseline turn-signal use from the designated final goal of 80% and then dividing by the number of weeks in the intervention phase (i.e., 5). The dynamic goal for the first week was the individual's baseline turn-signal use plus this incremental increase. Goals for subsequent weeks were raised by the incremental increase until the final week when the dynamic goal matched the final goal of 80%.

If a deliverer had a 30% baseline performance, for example, this was subtracted from 80% for a difference of 50 percentage points. This number was divided by five (i.e., the number of weeks in the intervention phase) for an incremental increase rate of 10 percentage points per week for five weeks. The deliverer's first week dynamic goal would, therefore, be 40% (i.e., 30% baseline plus 10 percentage points). Then the next week's goal would be 50% and would increase 10 percentage points until the final week (Week 5) goal of 80% would be set.

We calculated dynamic goals in this way to assure that both the static and dynamic groups would have the same final goal. This also allowed us to provide a dynamic goal that was customized to the individual deliverer. Also, the increases in dynamic goals over the five weeks of the intervention were small enough that they would seem to be more attainable than the much larger 80% goal.

Deliverers in the static/dynamic condition were assigned both weekly dynamic and static goals during the intervention period. In other words, they received both the 80% static goal as well as new weekly goals based on their personalized incremental increases over baseline. Hence, the drivers who received static and dynamic goals were told what was expected of them overall and what level of responding would keep them on a "pace" to achieve the overall goal in the time allotted.

The deliverers received their goals and individualized feedback in a private memorandum at the end of each week. Each memorandum had both a verbal and graphical representation of their goal(s) and percentage turn-signal use from the previous week(s) as well as their goal(s) and percentage turn-signal use for the current week. These personalized graphs were similar to the public goal and feedback graphs used in previous studies. At the end of the five-week intervention phase, a final memorandum was handed out to the drivers who were then told that the intervention was complete and no more goals would be set and no more feedback provided. Presentations of memos ceased and withdrawal observations continued for the next five weeks.

Results

Rather marked differences between deliverers' turn-signal use were evident across the three goal-setting interventions. Data plotted in Figure 19 shows turn-signal use for the static, dynamic, and static/dynamic groups. The static group increased slightly, from a baseline mean of 47% to an intervention mean of 49% and continued to increase during withdrawal to a mean of 57%. The dynamic group had a larger increase in turn-signal use from a baseline mean of 42% to an intervention mean of 58%, which was maintained during withdrawal at a mean of 53%. The static/dynamic group increased their turn-signal use substantially, from a baseline mean of 42% to an intervention mean of 70%, and then declined to a mean of 44% during withdrawal.

An examination of data plotted in Figure 19 reveals a pattern by the dynamic group in which turn-signal use initially decreased and then rose to a mean of 79% use by the final week of the intervention. This pattern is consistent with the successively more difficult goals they were given over the five weeks of the intervention. In contrast, the static group initially increased their turn-signal use to over 70% during the first week of the intervention. However, when they received the same goal during the second week, their turn-signal use decreased.

Implications

These findings offer some instructive insights into how static and dynamic goals may influence performance. Based on their review over 500 goal-setting studies, Locke and Latham (1990) concluded: (a) difficult yet attainable goals are the most effective; (b) the more specific a goal, the more it impacts performance; and (c) goal-setting paired with feedback is usually most influential. Our study had all three of Locke and Latham's suggested components, and all three groups increased their turn-signal use during the intervention phases. It is noteworthy, however, that none of the groups attained the final goal level of 80% mean turn-signal use.

In contrast to the static goal condition, dynamic goals were more frequent and referred to action nearer in time. Thus, dynamic goals offered more response information than static-only goals, because this frequent goal setting offered new goals rather than reiterating the same goals (as a reminder). This is consistent with the Behavior Change Taxonomy (Table 1) that suggests interventions with higher response information will result in greater behavioral impact. Dynamic goals also provided successive opportunities for "small wins" (Weick, 1984), which reinforced the deliverer's behavior more frequently than static goals, a process consistent with basic shaping principles (Geller, 1997; Martin & Pear, 1996). The increase by deliverers in the dynamic group suggests that this technique of setting goals is more effective than static goal setting.

The combination of static and dynamic goal-setting was the most effective technique in the current study. The added static goal put the dynamic goals in context with a final endpoint. Most drivers in the static/dynamic group probably recognized the "step" pattern of the

FIGURE 19. Percent weekly turn-signal use across baseline, individualized goal and feedback intervention, and withdrawal phases for the dynamic, static, and dynamic/static groups during Ludwig (1999).

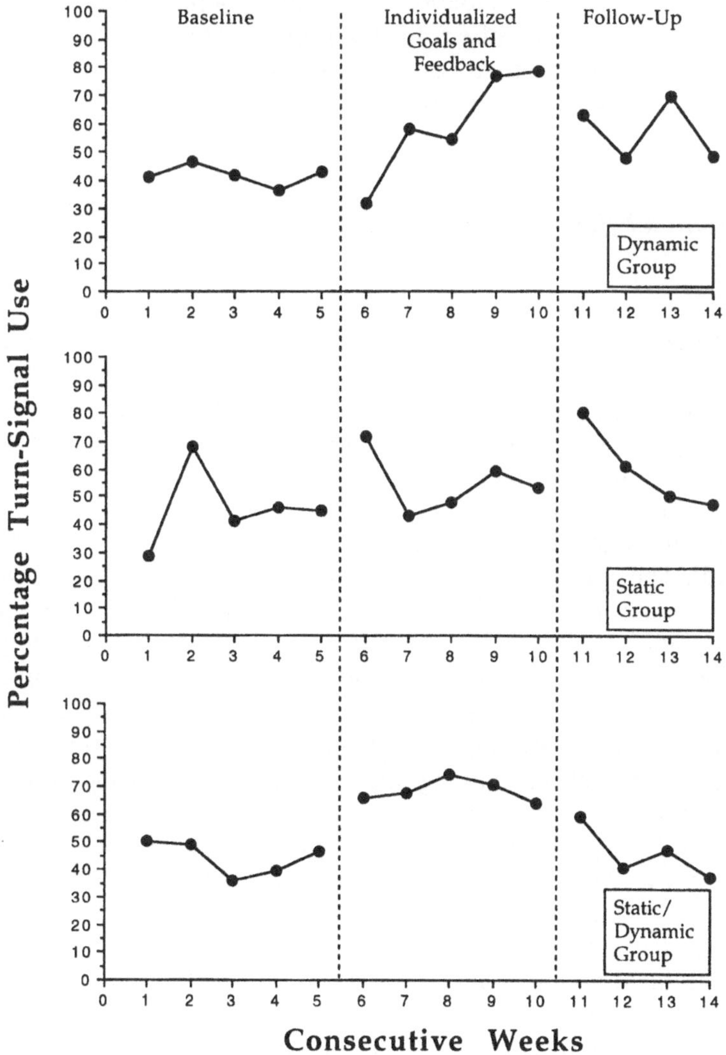

dynamic goals toward the ultimate static goal after the second week. The sequencing of proximal goals allowed the deliverers in this group to gauge their progress toward the final goal. If they stayed "in step" they would achieve the ultimate endpoint or static goal. A more parsimonious account for the superiority of this group is that the goal statements occurred most often. In this group, static goal statements were presented concurrent with every presentation of weekly feedback and new dynamic goal statements.

Generalization Effects

With regard to response generalization, the drivers who received static and dynamic goals had the greatest increases in non-targeted behaviors. Data plotted in Figure 20 show the percentage of complete stopping for the static, dynamic, and static/dynamic groups. The deliverers receiving the static goals did not show an increase in complete stopping, from a baseline mean of 38% to 39% complete stopping during the turn-signal intervention and 42% complete stopping during withdrawal. The dynamic group decreased its complete stopping from a baseline mean of 45% to 34% complete stopping during the intervention and then to a mean of 38% during withdrawal. The static/dynamic group increased its complete stopping from a baseline mean of 39% to 47% complete stopping during the intervention and then reversed to a mean of 39% during withdrawal. There were no notable changes in safety-belt use among any of the groups over the experimental phases.

These results suggest that the type of goal-setting used can influence changes in both target and non-target behaviors. The group that was exposed to the dynamic goals behaved in ways that suggested they engaged in some countercontrol by decreasing their complete stops during the turn-signal intervention. In contrast, the static/dynamic group's behavior provided no evidence of countercontrol; to the contrary, they actually increased their complete stopping during their turn-signal intervention. Thus, even though dynamic-only goals seem to work well on the targeted behavior, they may have been detrimental to non-targeted behaviors.

FIGURE 20. Percent weekly complete intersection stops across baseline, individualized goal and feedback intervention, and withdrawal phases for the dynamic, static, and dynamic/static groups during Ludwig (1999).

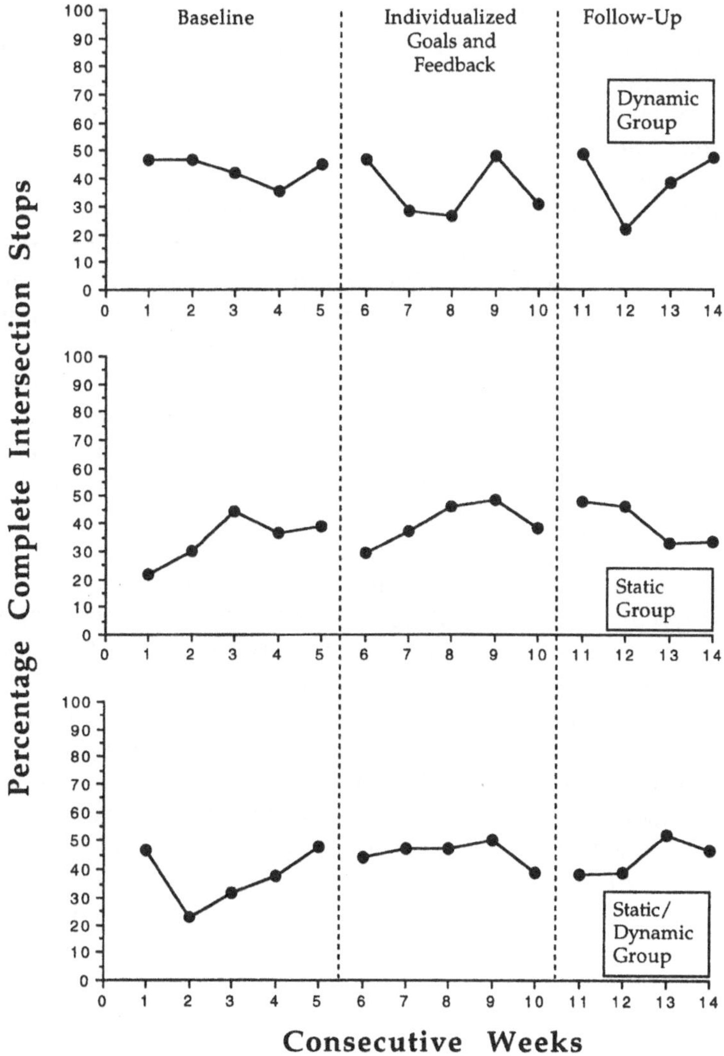

COMMUNITY AGENTS (LUDWIG & GELLER, 1999b)

The final study reviewed here describes how pizza deliverers respond when they were asked to promote safety-belt use in a community-wide promotion sponsored by their pizza delivery company. There is a clear distinction between the *participants* in an intervention and the *agents* of change that implement the intervention. Participants are the individual recipients of an intervention whose behavior is targeted for change. Agents of change are responsible for conducting the intervention and, as a result, become advocates of behavior change. The pizza deliverers in this study *became* agents of change. According to the MIL model, individuals influenced by previous interventions should become intervention agents themselves (cf. Katz & Lazarfeld, 1955). The higher agent-to-participant ratio achieved through using peers as agents to design and implement these interventions can, according to the MIL model, lead to more effective interventions.

When individuals adopt the role of a change agent, they are likely to promote the behavior among others in their social network. Because a whole store of pizza deliverers, cooks, dispatchers, and managers become intervention agents in a mutual effort to increase safety-belt use in their town, peer support was a factor in the intervention's impact. Intervention agents are also more apt to use indigenous contingencies (e.g., verbal reminders and reinforcers) in lieu of the more contrived contingencies created by external agents such as researchers. For this reason the Behavior Change Taxonomy predicts enrolling intervention agents will be an effective behavior change technique.

Cognitive dissonance theory (Festinger, 1957) suggests that when individuals' actions are inconsistent with their verbalizations (such as statements of intent), they are likely to change their behavior to bring it into greater conformity with their prior verbalizations. Thus, if intervention agents promote a behavior they don't currently perform, there is pressure to change–to bring personal behavior into compliance with the behavior advocated.

A behavior analytic interpretation of cognitive dissonance suggests that an inconsistency between intention and behavior creates an establishing operation that sets up conditions for negative reinforcement. Negative reinforcement occurs when the aversiveness of the situation is removed by bringing into agreement what one has said and what one does. Since it is possible the deliverers were being watched by the general public to see if they "practiced what they preached," it is likely some employees reminded themselves and others to buckle up.

The agents of community interventions for safety have usually been researchers conducting empirical studies (Geller, 1996; Geller, Johnson, & Pelton, 1982; Thyer, Geller, Williams, & Purcell, 1987). Nevertheless, some examples of successful community-based projects involved indigenous personnel as behavior change agents in industry (Johnson & Geller, 1980), a supermarket (Winett et al., 1991), a fast food restaurant (Cope & Geller, 1984), a university (Rudd & Geller, 1985), and a navy base (Kalsher, Geller, Clarke, & Lehman, 1989). However, none of these studies looked at whether the agents' behaviors also improved as a consequence of their involvement in the intervention.

Method

The pizza deliverers at Store A were enlisted to serve as agents of a community safety-belt campaign that targeted the community of the surrounding town in an ABA time series design. Store B was owned by a separate franchise in the same town as Store A and did not participate in the community program. After ten weeks of baseline observations, the safety-belt program was implemented for six weeks. Six weeks after the end of the intervention, follow-up observations began and were taken for six consecutive weeks. This was followed by an additional five-week break and another seven weeks of follow-up observations.

Intervention

The safety-belt campaign sponsored by Store A consisted of local radio and newspaper promotions. Customers received $1 off the price of their pizza if, while making their orders, they asked the dispatcher to remind the deliverer to buckle up. The dispatchers then printed a large "BU" on the receipt attached to the pizza box that deliverers refer to for the address of the customer. Thus, the deliverers saw the customer's reminder as they prepared to deliver the pizza (in this case, the customers were "agents of change").

Additionally, safety-belt reminder cards were pasted to the box tops of each pizza sold. These reminder cards were designed so customers could hang the cards on the rearview mirrors inside their vehicles. Customers whose reminder card was seen by local police officers, research assistants, or the deliverers themselves had their license-plate numbers reported to the participating radio station. Winners were randomly drawn and announced over the radio broadcast at a predetermined time. Winners could then stop by the radio station and receive a voucher for a free pizza.

Results and Generalization Effects

Figure 21 displays the safety-belt use observed for deliverers at Store A over the course of this study. Deliverers at Store A had a rather high safety-belt use prior to the intervention. This was most likely due to the fact that most deliverers at this store had been participants four months earlier in an awareness and promise-card program targeting safety-belt use (Ludwig & Geller, 1991). Nevertheless, Store A's safety-belt use rose 32% above baseline to a mean of 75% during the community safety-belt program and remained at this higher level throughout follow-up observations.

Data plotted in Figure 22 show turn-signal use of the pizza deliverers at Store A. Even though this behavior was not mentioned in any of the intervention operations, turn-signal use among deliverers increased 68% over baseline at Store A during the community safety-belt campaign and remained at this higher level throughout the follow-up phase.

Social Validity

Wolf (1978) and others (Geller, 1987; 1991b; Schwartz & Baer, 1991) have argued for the assessment of social validity when conducting applied behavioral research. Unfortunately, we did not directly assess whether safety-belt use increased in the community targeted by the pizza store's program. Nevertheless, we did perform an indirect assessment by conducting random phone interviews with residents of the community. When asked whether they were more likely to use their safety-belt because of the program, 58% of the 145 respondents answered "yes" while 25% said the program had not influenced their safety-belt use. When asked the questions "What percentage of the time do you buckle-up" and "What percentage of the time do you

FIGURE 21. Percent weekly safety-belt use across baseline, community program intervention, and follow-up phases for Store A during Ludwig and Geller (1999b).

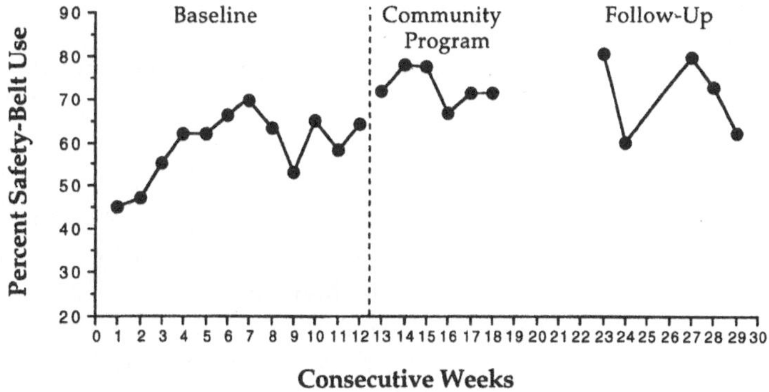

FIGURE 22. Percent weekly turn-signal use across baseline, community program intervention, and follow-up phases for Store A during Ludwig and Geller (1999b).

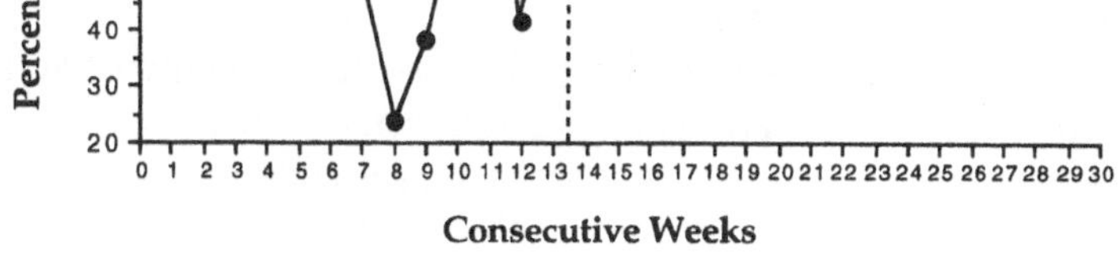

think pizza deliverers at (franchise name) buckle-up," most respondents said they were more likely to buckle-up than pizza deliverers by an average of 44 percentage points.

The community program was inexpensive to run and a feasible way for many businesses to support public health and safety. Advertisements were donated, and periodically the pizza store already offered $1-off coupons weekly in area newspapers. The pizza store gave away a retail value of $25 worth of pizzas to town citizens displaying their reminder cards, hardly a major corporate expense that was in fact, tax-deductible.

Implications

These results conform to predictions of the MIL model and Behavior Change Taxonomy (Geller et al., 1990; Geller & Ludwig, 1991). The increase in safety-belt use among the pizza delivery agents helped us confirm the notion that agents themselves will experience and exhibit beneficial changes in their own behavior as they are attempting to influence others. However, we should note that in many ways this intervention "stacked the deck" in our favor and may not have provided a fair test of the hypothesis. That is, the pizza deliverers also received a number of prompts for their own behavior. They were able to see the boxtop promotions with the safety-belt reminder card and therefore got a personalized reminder to buckle-up on their receipt. These reminders came from customers whom the deliverers then saw face-to-face after driving to their residence.

After the completion of the safety-belt intervention, there seemed to be some sustained beneficial effects among deliverers who participated in the program as well as among those deliverers who were hired afterwards (Geller & Ludwig, 1991). The maintenance of safety-belt use suggests the deliverers at Store A had adopted cultural practices that transcended the intervention through peer support and rule-governed behavior. The passage of a rule to a new member of a group is a defining feature of the concept of a cultural practice (Glenn, 1991; Redmon & Mason, in press).

The second author has researched a construct he named "actively caring" to characterize an array of practices that exemplify a culture in which peer support for safety is so prevalent it constitutes a "cultural norm" (Geller, 1991a, 1996). Thus, the maintenance of the results from the community campaign could be a result of an increase in the constellation of activities called actively caring among pizza deliverers as well as other store personnel.

LONG-TERM IMPACT OF MULTIPLE INTERVENTIONS

The collection of a large amount of behavioral data over an extended period of time is a hallmark of applied behavior analysis. The seven studies reviewed in this monograph presented data from behavioral observations that took place over a 10-year span. Approximately 140,000 behavioral observations were taken over this time including data collected from 881 different pizza deliverers, 437 of whom participated in an intervention program. Taken as a whole, these studies confirm that behavior-based intervention is a very effective method of increasing safe driving in an occupational setting. They also enabled us to study the impact that different ways of applying goal-setting and feedback techniques had on target behaviors and other safety-related behaviors.

Franchise A, North Carolina

Since we used some of the same pizza stores across studies, we were able to analyze long-term intervention impact and compare the influence of various intervention techniques. Data plotted in Figure 23 show the safety-belt use, turn-signal use, and complete stops for Franchise A in North Carolina. The deliverers in this store (with an average 78% turnover) experienced three different interventions. During the first baseline period, turn-signal use among deliverers at this store was less than 10%. The first intervention (Ludwig, Geller, & Clarke, 1999) targeted turn-signal use which more than doubled, and then stayed at this new level for the next 27 weeks. Then a second intervention (Ludwig, 1999) targeted complete stopping, yet increased turn-signal use to its highest point during the 65 weeks of field observations.

Complete stopping at this North Carolina store started below 20%, where it remained until the second intervention (Ludwig, Biggs, Wagner, & Geller, 1999) that targeted complete stopping. During this intervention's follow-up, increases in complete stopping were maintained and even increased to its highest point during the 65-week observation period. Safety-belt use was never targeted by an intervention at this store. Nevertheless, an upward pattern was noted over the 65 weeks of observation, with three intermittent interventions targeting turn-signal use and complete stopping.

Franchise B, North Carolina

Data plotted in Figure 24 show the safety-belt use, turn-signal use, and complete stops for Franchise B in North Carolina. The deliverers

FIGURE 23. Percent weekly safety-belt use, turn-signal use, and complete intersection stopping across 65 weeks for North Carolina Franchise A.

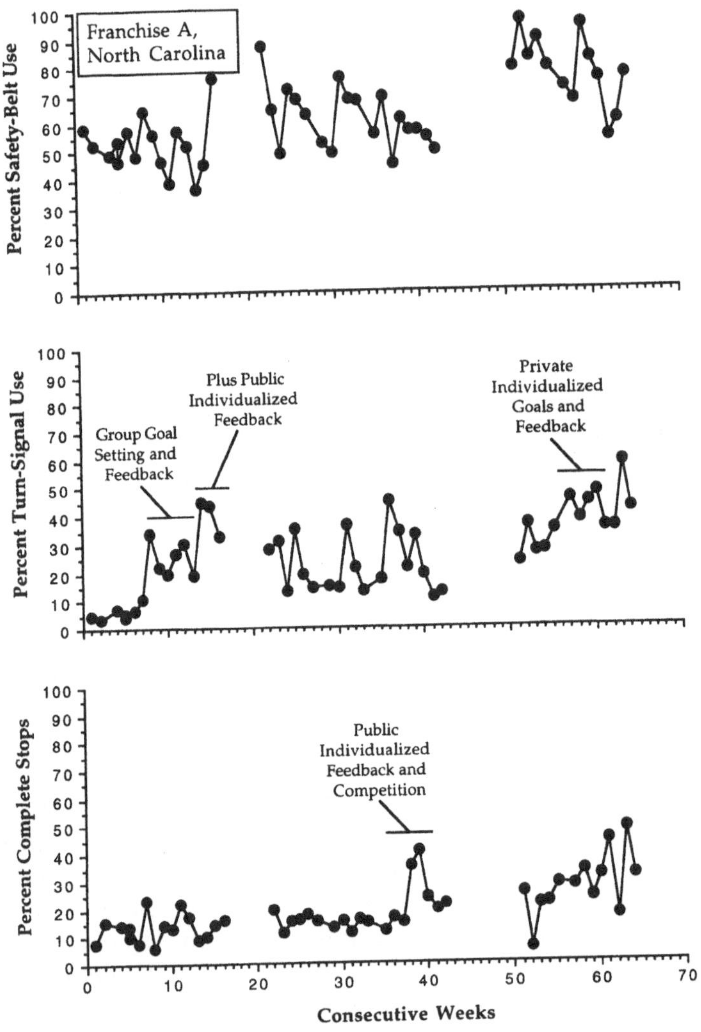

in this store, showing an average 66% turnover, also experienced three different interventions, all targeting turn-signal use. Turn-signal use among deliverers at this store began under 35%. The first intervention (Ludwig, Geller, & Clarke, 1999) increased turn-signal use temporarily. Then it returned to baseline levels until the second intervention (Ludwig, Biggs, Wagner, & Geller, 1999). Increases from the second intervention were maintained into the baseline of the third study (Ludwig, 1999); and then during the final intervention, it increased further to its highest point in 65 weeks. Complete stopping at this store remained at baseline levels throughout the 65 weeks of observation with the exception of transient increases during two of the turn-signal interventions. Like Franchise A, safety-belt use at Franchise B trended upward over 65 weeks.

Franchise C, North Carolina

Data plotted in Figure 25 show the safety-belt use, turn-signal use, and complete stops for Franchise C in North Carolina. The deliverers in this store averaged 57% turnover between studies and only experienced one intervention (Ludwig, 1999) which targeted turn-signal use after 58 weeks of baseline observations. Otherwise, this store was used as a comparison store for the other North Carolina stores. Turn-signal use among deliverers at this store remained relatively stable for 60 weeks, and then increased prominently during the Ludwig (1999) intervention. Complete stopping at this store remained relatively stable throughout the entire 65 weeks. Unlike the other franchises, safety-belt use among deliverers at Franchise C began at a very high level and decreased over the 65 weeks.

Franchise A, Virginia

Franchise A in Virginia was the only store that was observed across all of our studies. This gave us a unique opportunity to track certain safety behaviors at one site over a 10-year period. Data plotted in Figure 26 show the safety-belt use, turn-signal use, and complete stops at this store. With an average of 68% turnover, the deliverers experienced four interventions over a 3-year period. Then it was used as a comparison for Franchise A in North Carolina for the final 65 weeks.

Safety-belt use began below 45% during the initial Baseline phase

FIGURE 24. Percent weekly safety-belt use, turn-signal use, and complete intersection stopping across 65 weeks for North Carolina Franchise B.

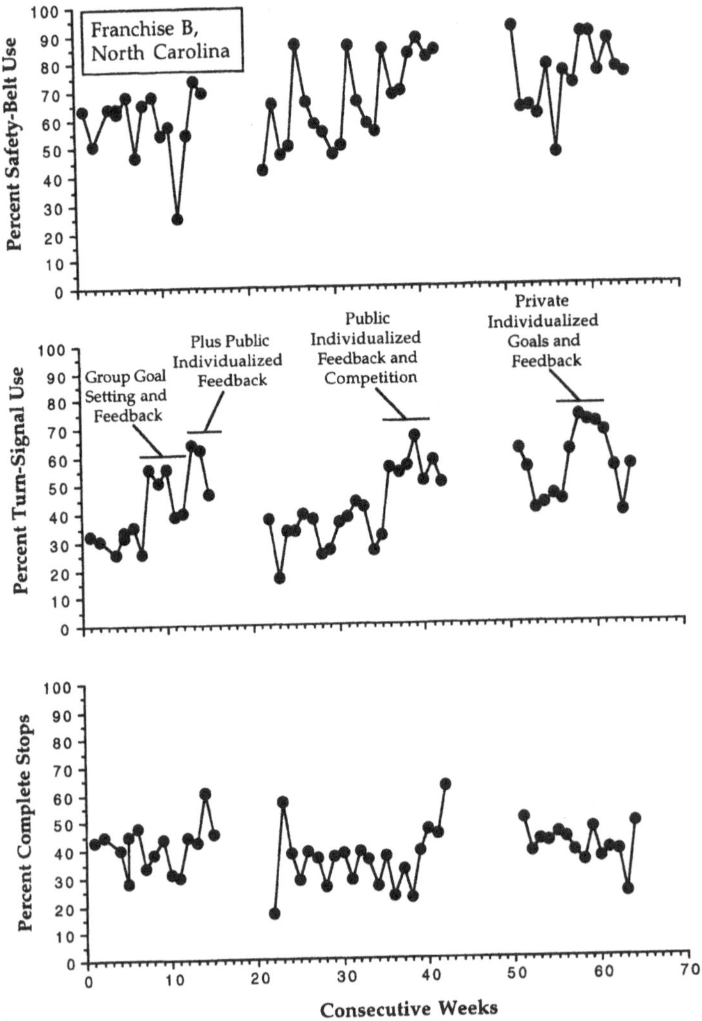

and nearly doubled during the first intervention (Ludwig & Geller, 1991). Then, safety-belt use reversed back down to baseline for only two weeks (corresponding with a Christmas holiday season when many deliverers were not present), returned close to the prior intervention levels, and then continued to increase during and after the com-

FIGURE 25. Percent weekly safety-belt use, turn-signal use, and complete intersection stopping across 65 weeks for North Carolina Franchise C.

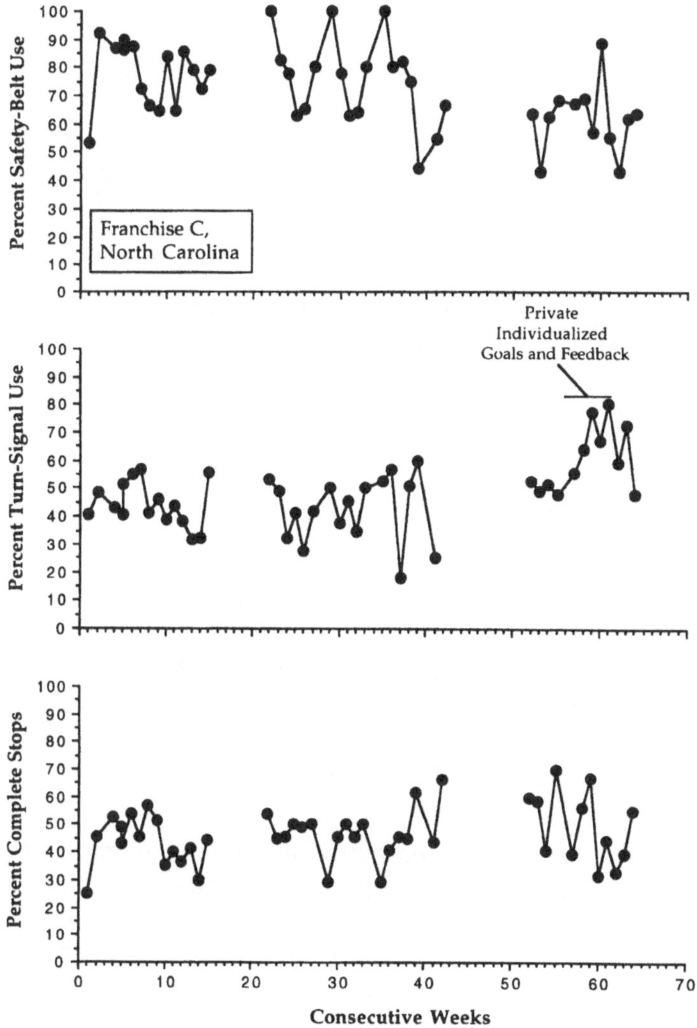

munity program (Ludwig & Geller, 1999b). During this time, data on turn-signal use revealed a general upward trend, with notable increases during the safety-belt interventions.

Approximately 60 weeks from the beginning of our first baseline observations, the national chain associated with Franchise A in Virgin-

FIGURE 26. Percent weekly safety-belt use, turn-signal use, and complete intersection stopping across multiple years for Virginia Franchise A.

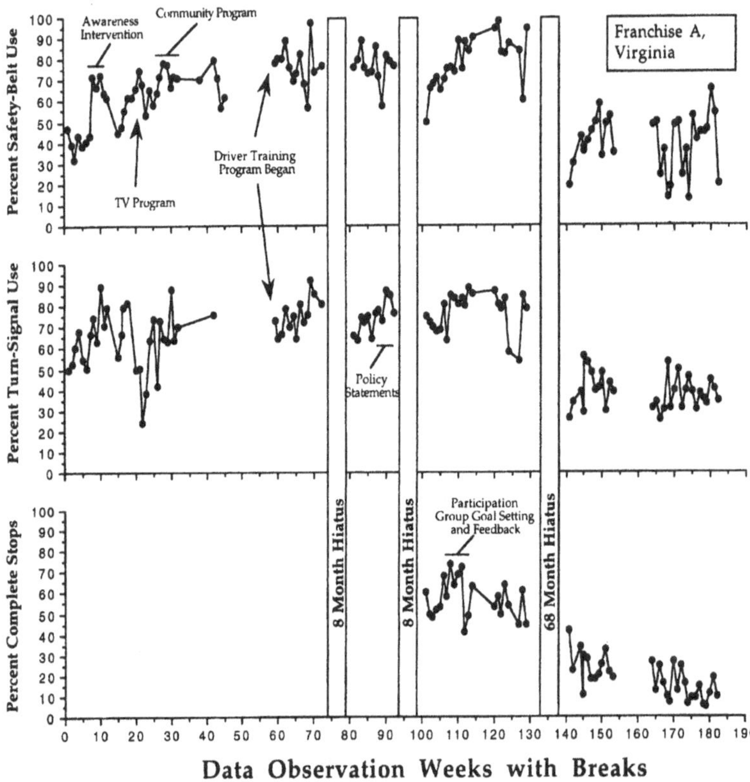

ia implemented a program to promote safe driving among its deliverers. This program included a 95-minute video and workbook designed by Geller and Kalsher (Domino's Pizza, 1989). It was disseminated to all franchise stores throughout the United States and Canada. The workbook followed the programmed instruction methodology devised by Keller (1968) to systematically cover a number of behaviors involved in safe driving including: driving speed, complete stops, vehicle-following distance, passing, merging, backing, yielding to pedestrians, using signals, using safety-belts, and vehicle maintenance.

The impact of the corporate driving education class on two behaviors (i.e., safety-belt and turn-signal use) at Franchise A in Virginia is also shown. Both safety-belt and turn-signal use were higher after the driving safety program. During the first month of the driver education program, safety-belt use averaged 78%, increasing from a baseline mean of 65%. It should be noted that the store had completed the community program only a month before baseline observations began and only 3 months before the education program was implemented. Safety-belt use remained high during the next couple of months. Turn-signal use did not show a substantial increase, from a baseline mean of 72% to an average of 74% following the driver education program.

After an 8-month hiatus, we resumed data collection at Franchise A in Virginia for the turn-signal policy interventions. Another 8-month hiatus followed before our observers started collecting data on complete intersection stopping. Deliverers in this franchise made up the participation group in the group goal-setting and feedback intervention (Ludwig & Geller, 1997). During this study safety-belt and turn-signal use continued to climb to all-time highs.

From the beginning of our observations at this franchise the use of safety belts and turn signals had increased substantially and remained consistently above 75% going into the 68-month hiatus. During this 5.75-year period, no safety interventions were conducted and all three behaviors (i.e., complete stopping, safety-belt, and turn-signal use) were down substantially when we resumed our field observations. Turn-signal use and complete intersection stopping were below the baseline averages measured when we started observations. During the final 65 weeks, Franchise A in Virginia was used as a comparison group with no intervention activity. Consequently, there were no upward trends in safety-belt or turn-signal use over this time. In addition, complete intersection stopping declined over this period.

Implications

These cross-study figures make it clear that some interventions conducted in previous studies had a lasting influence on driver behavior, even though many of the drivers who were present during the intervention were replaced. Although the external intervention operations were withdrawn, they may have been replaced by more indigenous safety operations taken from the original intervention or created separately on the part of the employees or management who became more aware of certain safety issues as a result of the earlier interventions. Secondly, it has been argued that organizational culture factors which Clayton, Mawhinney, Luke, and Cook (1997) call metacontingencies (e.g., peer and managerial support; cf. Geller, 1998a) can create reinforcing contingencies for behaviors consistent with the rest of a group's behavior or punishing contingencies for behaviors which are inconsistent. If a previous intervention was successful at increasing and maintaining safe driving, as well as related verbal behavior during on-the-job conversations, then new employees will enter an organization with drivers who model a higher prevalence of safe behaviors and probably promote those behaviors verbally.

It is also noteworthy that the prevalence of safe driving continued to increase with each subsequent intervention, especially when the intervention facilitated peer support and involvement. These findings support propositions of the MIL model. The sequence of interventions in each of the figures above progress from store-wide, low intrusive interventions (e.g., awareness sessions) to more intrusive interventions at the group level (e.g., group goal-setting and feedback), and then to very intrusive personalized interventions (e.g., public and private individualized feedback). Even though the same deliverers were not present across these various intervention programs, it is evident that implementation produced successively higher levels of the safety-related behaviors observed.

The roles of differential reinforcement can shape up behavior repertoires using, for example, intermittent schedules of reinforcement to maintain behavior over the long term. We would expect these to eventually extinguish unless reinforced further. On the other hand, if the shaping process creates reinforcement contingencies that outlive the intervention itself, then the contingencies can be "institutionalized" and maintain behavior indefinitely.

HISTORY EFFECTS

Also evident when viewing the time-series data in these figures is that events other than our interventions had substantial impact on the driving practices of the pizza deliverers. Often field-based research must rule out the potential impact of "history" effects caused by events independent of the intervention. This is quite evident when working with driving behavior because there are frequent public and within-organization attempts to increase safe driving. A notable example of this occurred when we were collecting baseline data for our community-based study (Ludwig & Geller, 1999b).

About a month after we introduced baseline observations at Franchise A in Virginia, an *Inside Edition* broadcast was aired which accused the national company of managerial practices that encouraged unsafe driving. It also provided graphic accounts of civilians getting killed by deliverers for this company, and it outlined the lawsuits that resulted. Data plotted in Figure 26 show the impact of this broadcast (depicted by an arrow) on both safety-belt and turn-signal use. The impact was short-lived and it was fortuitous that this event took place during our baseline observations. If it had occurred during an intervention, we may have mistakenly attributed the increase to our treatment. This same company implemented their nationwide driver education program the following year. Because of this potential contamination, we had to cancel all planned interventions for this franchise. Obviously, our interventions and associated cultural changes were not the only events that influenced driving safety among the pizza deliverers.

Another important variable that can influence safe driving is the physical environment where driving occurs. There are contexts (e.g., streets empty of other vehicles) in which risky driving is less likely to result in a punishing outcome such as a vehicle crash, and there are contexts (e.g., wet, slippery streets) in which risky driving is more likely to result in a punishing outcome. An analysis of these stimulus events can provide insight into driving situations more or less impervious to a behavior change intervention.

STIMULUS EVENTS

Stimulus events (Bijou & Baer, 1961) are antecedents (i.e., the presence, absence or change of a stimulus) that increase the likelihood that specific behaviors will follow. In contrast, setting events (e.g., fatigue from driving all night) are more general, are not necessarily contiguous with a target behavior, and may influence a wide range of behaviors (Wahler & Fox, 1981). Stimulus events are associated with consequences through differential reinforcement. If a response is often punished in the presence of a particular stimulus event then that response is less likely to occur in the presence of that stimulus event in the future. Therefore stimulus events can result in large differences in behavioral responding.

Weather

Weather can be considered a stimulus event. It stands to reason that the likelihood of certain safe driving behaviors increase in rain and snow, as opposed to clear weather. This is because these driving conditions may have been associated with punishing consequences (e.g., losing control of a vehicle, wrecking a vehicle, and/or getting injured) sometime in an individual's driving history. To evaluate this, our observers noted the weather conditions (i.e., clear, rain, or snow) present during data collection session. During our seven studies, 98,490 baseline observations were made in clear weather, 10,390 in rain, and 990 in snow.

Table 4 shows the percentages of safe-driving behaviors across various weather conditions. Deliverers used their safety-belt an average of 56% of the time in clear weather, 67% of the time in the rain, and 76% of the time in snow. As the road conditions became more hazardous, deliverers were more likely to protect themselves with a safety-belt. There were no differences in turn-signal use associated with these weather conditions. Deliverers used their turn-signal an average of 38% of the time in clear weather, 34% of the time in the rain, and 33% of the time in snow. Thus, if anything, there was slightly less turn-signal use in inclement weather than on clear days.

The pattern of complete stopping at intersections demonstrated a more complex relationship. Deliverers came to a complete stop substantially more often in rain (49%) than in clear weather (33%). However, deliverers came to a complete stop substantially less in snow (i.e., only 23% of the time). This suggests that snow prompts less complete stopping, presumably because it is associated with sliding when the brake pedal is depressed. These results are difficult to generalize to the greater population because they were collected in towns with populations of approximately 35,000 in the Appalachian mountain chain and included only pizza deliverers, most of whom have relatively few years of driving experience in adverse conditions. Nevertheless, our observations suggest weather conditions were stimulus events for most drivers.

Turn Direction and Traffic

Because stimulus events can have a substantial impact on driving behavior, they need to be considered when assessing intervention impact. If a stimulus event increases the likelihood of a targeted be-

TABLE 4. Mean Safety-Belt Use, Turn-Signal Use, and Complete Intersection Stops as a Function of Weather Conditions Across Sites in North Carolina and Virginia

Weather Condition	Safety-Belt Use	Turn-Signal Use	Complete Stops
Clear	56%	38%	33%
Rain	67%	34%	49%
Snow	76%	33%	23%

havior, then it's more difficult to isolate the independent impact of an intervention designed to increase the frequency of that behavior. Therefore, the impact of an intervention can best be evaluated in the absence of that antecedent. For example, the direction one is turning out of an intersection can influence stopping behavior. When we analyzed turn-signal use, it was significantly lower when the deliverer was making a right turn (i.e., 56%) than when making a left turn (i.e., 76%). Likewise, traffic patterns probably influence the frequency of complete stopping and turn-signal use. In our studies, for example, a pizza deliverer making a turn was 528% less likely to come to a complete stop before making a right turn with no traffic than a left turn with traffic present.

We examined how these stimulus events influence deliverers' responsiveness to our interventions by calculating the percentage of complete stops and turn signal use among pizza deliverers when making left versus right turns in traffic or without traffic. We defined "traffic" as any other vehicle within 100 ft. of intersecting with the vehicle being observed. Our inter-rater reliability (i.e., percent agreement) for traffic condition observations was 82% agreement.

Data plotted in Figure 27 show the impact of the intervention that targeted turn-signal use for each direction turned (i.e., right or left turn) at Stores A and B during the Ludwig, Biggs, Wagner, and Geller (1999) study. Baseline observations at Store A revealed deliverers used their turn-signal 31 percentage points more and came to a complete stop 14 percentage points more when turning left than when turning right. Oddly, baseline observations at Store B revealed the fact that turn-signal use was 10 percentage points lower when turning left than when turning right, while complete intersection stops were 18 percentage points higher when turning left than when turning right. This is possibly due to another stimulus event: road configuration.

FIGURE 27. Percent turn-signal use while making a right or left turn during baseline, intervention, and withdrawal phases of Ludwig, Biggs, Wagner, and Geller (1999).

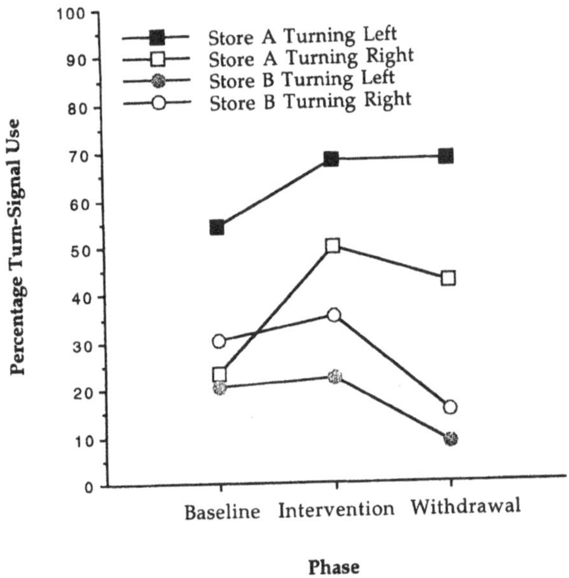

Store A's deliverers had to cross two lanes of traffic to make a left turn, while Store B exited onto a side street with only one lane of traffic. The impact of the intervention on turn-signal use at Store A seemed to be more pronounced for right than left turns. However, this could be because of the already high use of left turn-signals during baseline at this store.

Data plotted in Figure 28 show mean percentage of deliverers using their turn-signals at Stores A and B for traffic and non-traffic conditions. During baseline at Store A, deliverers used their turn-signal 14 percentage points more often and came to a complete stop 53 percentage points more often when turning in traffic than in no traffic. During baseline at Store B, deliverers used their turn-signal 11 percentage points more often and came to a complete stop 29 percentage points more often when turning in traffic than in no traffic. The impact of the intervention on turn-signal use at Store A and on complete intersection stopping at Store B seemed to be equivalent for both traffic and non-

FIGURE 28. Percent turn-signal use while making a turn in traffic or no traffic during baseline, intervention, and withdrawal phases of Ludwig, Biggs, Wagner, and Geller (1999).

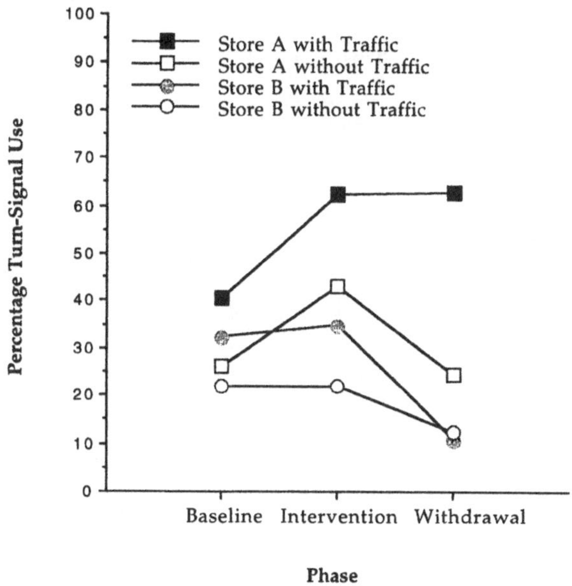

traffic conditions. However, the observations at Store A suggest that turn-signal use remained near intervention levels (i.e., maintenance) during the withdrawal phase when traffic was present at the time of the turn.

Figures 29 and 30 depict the impact of the turn-signal intervention on complete intersection stopping when examined separately for turn direction and traffic conditions, respectively. Figure 29 suggests a decrease in complete stopping among deliverers at Store A while making a left turn during the intervention phase. Figure 30 also provides evidence of a substantial decrease in complete stopping among deliverers at Store A when turning into traffic during their turn-signal intervention.

This demonstration of countercontrol in response to the competition intervention in the Ludwig, Biggs, Wagner, and Geller (1999) study is somewhat alarming in that a left turn into traffic is the most dangerous turn to make. Breaking down the data into traffic and turn direction conditions allows us to get a more sensitive measure of these occur-

FIGURE 29. Percent complete stopping while making a right or left turn during baseline, intervention, and withdrawal phases of Ludwig, Biggs, Wagner, and Geller (1999).

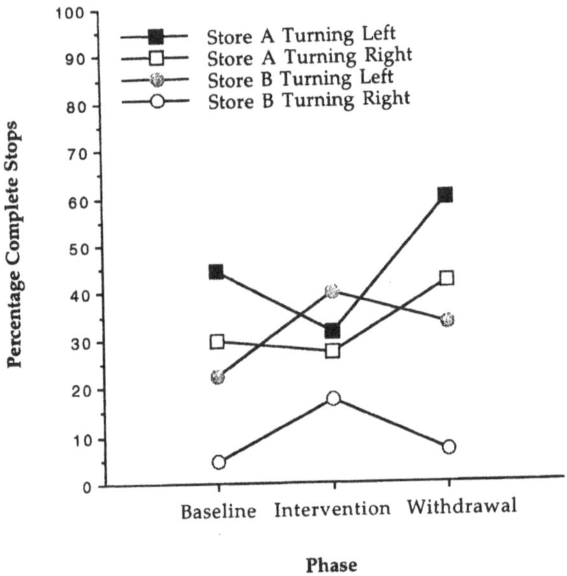

rences. Actually, the incidents of stopping during right turns in low traffic were already low and therefore a "floor" effect may have prevented the same intervention effect with right as with left turns.

RESPONSE GENERALIZATION

On several occasions we have invoked the concept of "response generalization" when interpreting the beneficial effects of driving safety interventions on a non-targeted behavior (Ludwig & Geller, 1991, 1997, 1999a, b; Ludwig, Geller, & Clarke, 1999; Ludwig, Biggs, Wagner, & Geller, 1999). Response generalization is a spread of effect to behaviors similar in typography, form, or function. This is analogous to the spread of effect phenomena associated with stimulus generalization. We presume these intervention programs caused a ". . . spread of effect . . . to other responses not included in the reinforced class . . ." (Catania, 1979).

FIGURE 30. Percent complete stopping while making a turn in traffic or no traffic during baseline, intervention, and withdrawal phases of Ludwig, Biggs, Wagner, and Geller (1999).

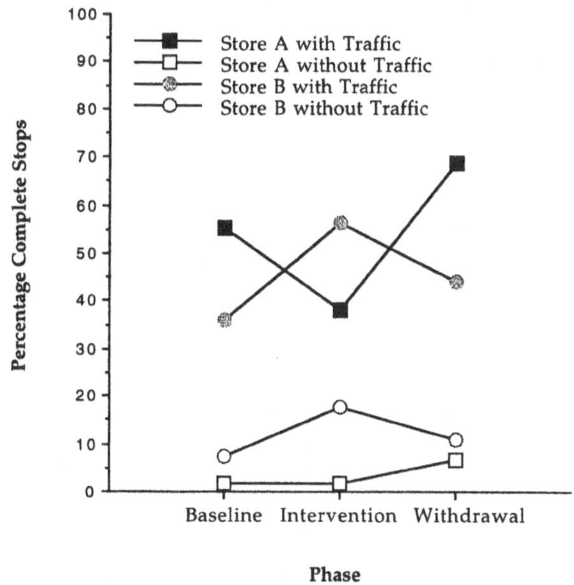

Several researchers have used response generalization to refer to treatment effects analogous to those we have shown here with non-targeted safety-related behaviors (e.g., Burleigh & Marholin, 1977; Coleman, 1974; Kazdin, 1973; McLeskey, Rieth, & Polsgrove, 1980; Warren, Baer, & Rogers-Warren, 1979; Winkel, 1987). However, a seminal publication on generalization by Stokes and Baer (1977) sidestepped the "controversy concerning terminology" (p. 350), and asked the reader to consider a temporary definition of generalization across behaviors. In reality, response generalization may only be one of many descriptions for the co-occurrence of different behaviors. To group all descriptions under the rubric of "generalization" might not only be confusing, but it could limit theory development and intervention improvement.

Willems (1974) and others, arguing from a behavioral ecology perspective (e.g., Eisenberg, 1972; Rogers-Warren & Warren, 1977), challenged applied researchers to anticipate second- and third-order consequences of interventions before implementation. By describing the functional ecosystem in which the target behavior occurs, they suggested researchers could better understand the interrelationships among behaviors and the naturally controlling conditions apart from direct (and often contrived) contingencies. A first step is to probe for correlations between behaviors. This can be assessed with a correlation coefficient. However, when many behaviors are observed over relatively long periods of time, factor and cluster analyses can be applied (Voeltz & Evans, 1982; Wahler, 1975), as well as multiple regression (Martens & Witt, 1984).

Correlations

Notable efforts have been made to study existing interrelationships between correlated response patterns (e.g., Voelts & Evans, 1982; Wahler, 1975; Wahler & Fox, 1980, 1981). Likewise, we found a rather consistent pattern of Pearson correlations across our observed behaviors. For example, baseline correlations between safety-belt and turn-signal use were .53 ($p < .05$) in Ludwig, Biggs, Wagner, and Geller (1999), .42 ($p < .05$) in Ludwig and Geller (1991), and .43 ($p < .05$) in Ludwig and Geller (1997).

We also found a consistent relationship between complete intersection stops and turn-signal use. Baseline correlations between complete intersection stops and turn-signal use were .44 ($p < .05$) in Ludwig, Biggs, Wagner, and Geller (1999), and .40 ($p < .05$) in Ludwig and Geller (1997). In contrast, we did not observe a statistically significant relationship between safety-belt use and complete intersection stops. For example, baseline correlations between safety-belt use and complete intersection stops were .10 ($p > .05$) in Ludwig, Biggs, Wagner, and Geller (1999) and .19 ($p > .05$) in Ludwig and Geller (1997). It is interesting that turn-signal use correlates significantly with both complete stopping and safety-belt use, while complete stopping and safety-belt use do not covary significantly.

It seems that different contingencies and response histories maintain complete stopping and safety-belt use. And turn-signal use is at least partially maintained by both sets of contingencies. The use of safety-belts and turn-signals may be linked because they engage devices in the car not required for the actual operation of the vehicle. Rather they represent extra behaviors used by a driver to increase safety while operating the vehicle. The brake pedal, on the other hand, is a device used for vehicle operation. Therefore, we would expect complete stopping to be more correlated with maintaining a certain vehicle speed and less related to uses of safety belts and turn signals. This helps explain the low correlation between safety-belt use and complete stopping.

As suggested earlier, turn-signal use may be a part of a response chain linked to complete stopping when a driver approaches an intersection. Even though signaling a turn is not essential for operating a vehicle, it is often paired with complete stopping and may be functionally related to safe intersection behaviors. However, the observation that certain behaviors are correlated during naturalistic observations cannot establish that these behaviors are functionally related to some shared set of antecedents and consequences. So our explanation here can only be conjecture at this point.

Changing Correlations

The next step in assessing response generalization is to show that these correlations change in predictable ways when one of the behaviors is targeted by an intervention. Pigott, Fantuzzo, and Gorsuch (1987) suggest using a scatterplot to analyze the correlation between baseline and post-baseline observations. If the behaviors are related, the correlation between behaviors will approximate a linear relationship during both baseline and intervention phases. Assuming that only one behavior was targeted by the intervention, these results would indicate a change in one behavior (i.e., the target) was associated with a commensurate change in the second. If there is no apparent correlation during the baseline phase but then a correlation is found during the intervention, the intervention apparently strengthened the relationship between the behaviors.

Ludwig and Geller (1991) compared the correlation of safety-belt and turn-signal use before and after the awareness and promise-card intervention. The correlation was .42 during baseline but decreased dramatically during the intervention phase to .08. However, both safety-belt use, which was targeted by the intervention, and turn-signal use increased during the intervention phase.

Data plotted in Figure 31 are scatterplots that graphically depict the relationship between safety-belt and turn-signal use. The white squares represent the relationship during baseline. Individuals who were more likely to use their belt were also more likely to use their turn-signal. Therefore, a moderate correlation is apparent.

FIGURE 31. Scatterplots showing the correlation between safety-belt and turn-signal use during baseline and intervention phases of Ludwig and Geller (1991). Open squares represent baseline data and filled squares represent intervention-phase data.

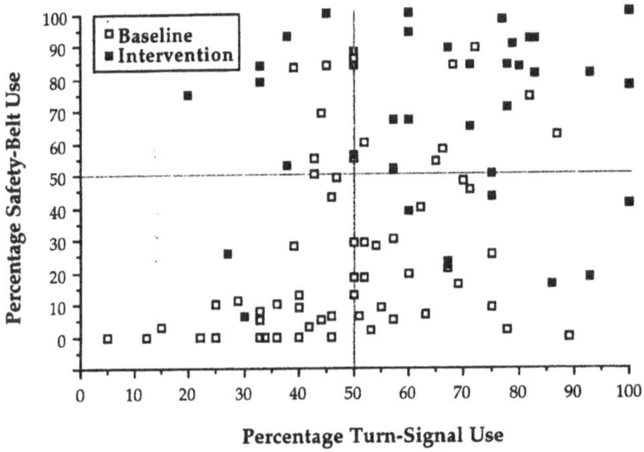

The black squares in Figure 31 represent the relationship between safety-belt and turn-signal use during the intervention phase. Many more individual data points appear in the upper right quadrant of this scatterplot, demonstrating that the deliverers not only increased their safety-belt use but also increased their use of turn-signals. Also, because the majority of data points during the intervention are in the one upper-right quadrant, it is probable the correlation was truncated by range restriction and not because of some operation of the intervention.

Ludwig, Biggs, Wagner, and Geller (1999) reported similar reductions in response correlations from baseline to an intervention involving competitive rewards and feedback. Baseline correlations of deliverers' safety-belt use, turn-signal use, and complete intersection stops were conducted across the three experimental phases of baseline, intervention, and withdrawal. The correlation between safety-belt and turn-signal use during baseline was .53 ($p < .05$). This correlation decreased during the intervention phase to .09 ($p > .05$), and remained low during withdrawal ($r = .18, p > .05$).

The correlation between complete intersection stops and turn-signal use during baseline was .44 ($p < .05$). The correlation decreased during the intervention phase to .13 ($p > .05$) and remained low during the withdrawal phase ($r = .13, p > .05$). The correlation between complete intersection stops and safety-belt use was not significant during the baseline ($r = .10, p > .05$), intervention ($r = -.19, p > .05$), or withdrawal phases ($r = .08, p > .05$). Scatterplot analyses reveal that, akin to our conclusions about the change in correlations in the Ludwig and Geller (1991) study, a ceiling effect caused range restriction and thereby reduced the correlation coefficient.

We completed a more extensive analysis of the inter-relatedness of these behaviors for the participation group in the Ludwig and Geller (1997) study which targeted complete intersection stopping with group goals and feedback. We looked at time-lag Pearson correlations (i.e., comparing correlations across time) based on the percentage of times a deliverer was observed engaging in each behavior during the baseline and intervention phases. In Figure 32 data for individual deliverers are plotted with respect to percentage complete stops and percentages turn-signal use graphically depiciting a non-significant correlation during baseline ($r = .11$ $p > .05$) and a significant correlation during the intervention $r = .40, p <.05$). The linear regression line (of "best fit") demonstrated the change in relationship between these two behaviors as a function of phase. During baseline, turn-signal use and complete stopping appear to be unrelated. However, during the intervention phase a positive relationship was found. What is apparent in the scatterplot is a shift in the relationship from the middle of the graph to the upper right quadrant. This illustrates response generalization. As complete stops increased following the intervention that targeted this behavior, so did drivers' use of turn signals.

To depict more clearly the phenomenon of response generalization, the scatterplots in the previous figure were superimposed in Figure 33, and individuals were tracked from one phase to the other. Dark circles represent the baseline data of selected deliverers who had at least a 10 percentage-point increase in turn-signal use during the intervention phase. Dark squares represent the intervention observations for these same drivers. Because these subjects were observed during both the baseline and intervention phases, it was possible to link these two segments of data. An arrow is provided to connect individual data from the baseline phase to the intervention phase. For these deliverers it appears the effect of the intervention generalized to turn-signal use.

Data representing the rest of the Participation group during the Intervention phase are represented by white squares.

Data plotted in Figure 34 show, in dark circles, the relationship between individual percentages of complete stops and safety-belt use during baseline, specifically for subjects who had a 10 percentage-point increase in safety-belt use from baseline to intervention. All but one of the subjects who were observed to use their safety-belt more than 50% of the time during the baseline phase exhibited dramatic response generalization characterized by movement toward the upper right of the graph. With the exception of one, subjects who rarely used their safety-belts during the baseline phase did not show any improvement in their mean percentage of complete stops during the intervention phase.

The time-lag correlations discussed above appear to confirm instances of response generalization by showing how the relationships between targeted and non-targeted behaviors changed across baseline and intervention phases. They are consistent with the longitudinal criteria for estimating indirect effects suggested by Gollob and Reichardt (1991). However, Gollob and Reichardt recommend that "Other things being equal, the more time points between Time 1 and Time 2 at which X (independent variable: intervention), Y (direct effect:

FIGURE 32. Scatterplots showing the correlation between complete stopping and turn-signal use during baseline and intervention phases of Ludwig and Geller (1997). Each open square represents data from an individual deliverer.

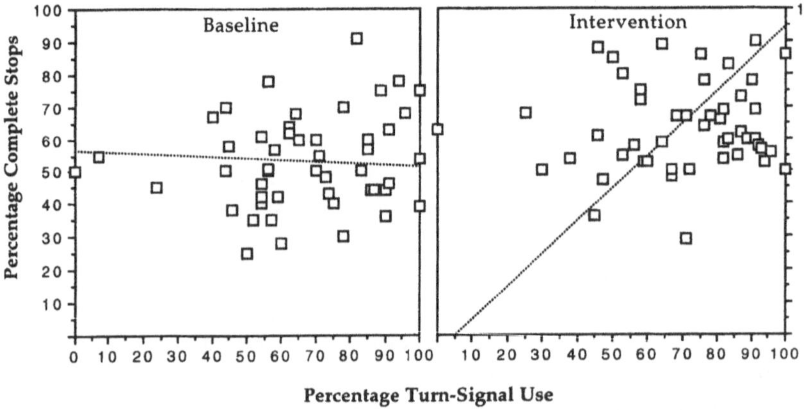

FIGURE 33. Scatterplots linking individual complete stopping and turn-signal use across baseline and intervention phases of Ludwig and Geller (1997). Filled circles represent data from selected deliverers during baseline. Open squares represent data from individual deliverers during the intervention phase. Arrows link selected deliverers' data across baseline and intervention phases.

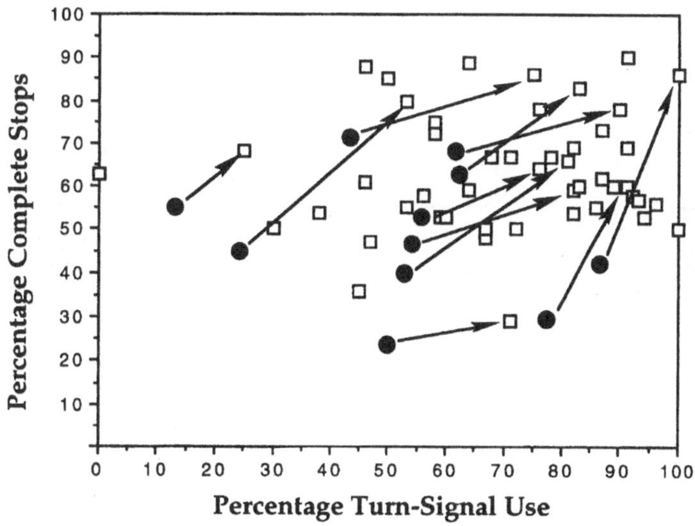

complete intersection stopping), and Z (indirect effect: non-targeted behaviors) are measured, the better the estimates of the size of the overall direct and indirect effects" (p. 259; parentheses added).

The longitudinal time series analysis of response generalization that have appeared throughout this monograph (i.e., Figures 5, 9, 10, 13, 14, 15, 17, 20, and 22) provide ample evidence in support of the point made by Gollob and Reichardt. However, the process of aggregating data across groups obscures the fact that, in the presence of the same intervention, some individuals exhibit generalization while others do not.

Generalization Effects in Individuals

An experimental analysis of group behavior can only suggest the possibility of a behavioral process such as response generalization. It is the behavior of individuals, not groups, that generalize. Individual generalization was shown in the arrow-enhanced scatterplots depicted

FIGURE 34. Scatterplots linking individual complete stopping and safety-belt use across baseline and intervention phases of Ludwig and Geller (1997). Filled circles represent data from selected deliverers during baseline. Open squares represent data from individual deliverers during the intervention phase. Arrows link selected deliverers' data across baseline and intervention phases.

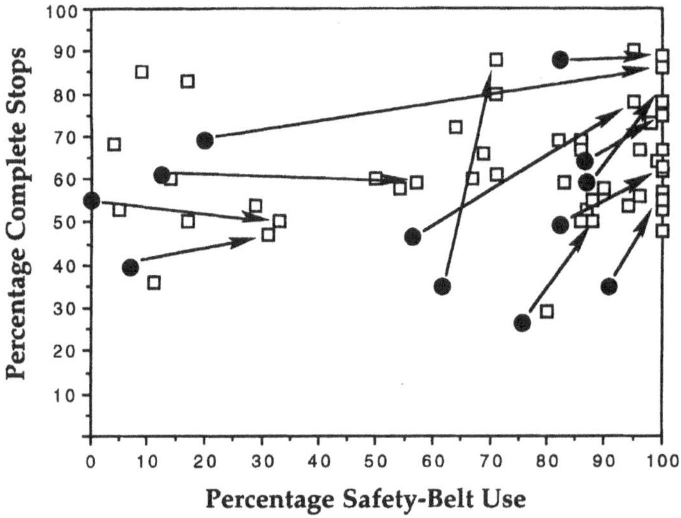

above. However, these presentations do not allow us to see the individual variation in non-targeted behaviors before, during, and after the intervention.

The following figures show weekly complete stopping percentages for individual deliverers during the dual-intervention study (Ludwig, Geller, & Clarke, 1999) that targeted turn signals. Each data point represents a week of observations for a particular deliverer. Weeks where a particular deliverer was observed less than six times were not graphed. The first intervention involved a group goal and feedback, followed by a second intervention that added public individual feedback. Complete stopping was not targeted nor mentioned in the intervention operations. Changes in stopping behavior concurrent with these two interventions provide evidence of response generalization.

Individual deliverers depicted in Figure 35 increased their complete stopping over their baseline during the group goal and feedback inter-

FIGURE 35. Percent weekly complete stopping across baseline, group goal-setting and feedback intervention, public individualized feedback intervention, and follow-up phases for individuals during Ludwig, Geller, and Clarke (1999).

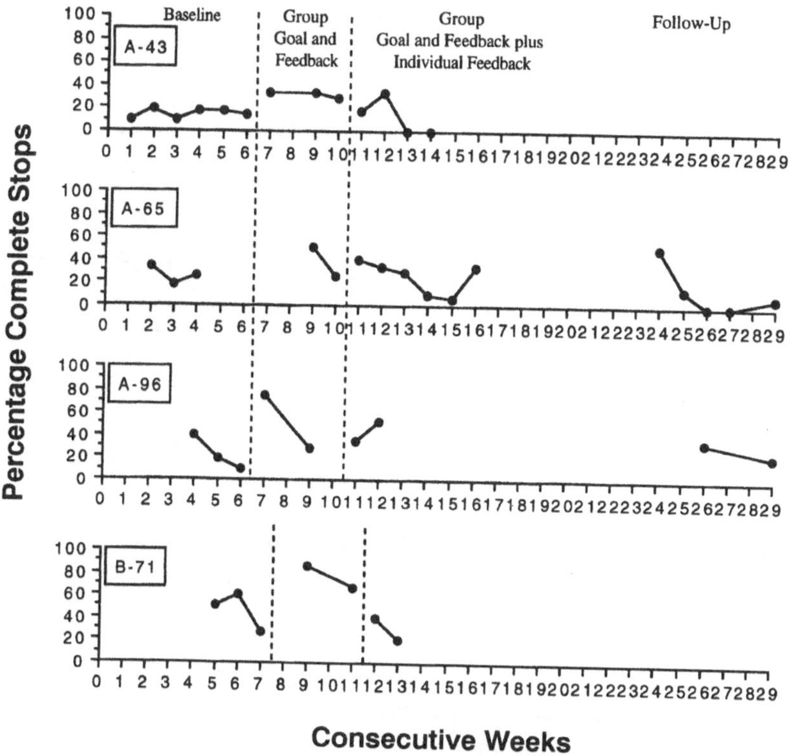

vention. No further increases during the individual feedback phase were observed and some decreased their complete stopping during this phase. Driver A-43 had a relatively stable baseline of 17% complete stopping. During the group turn-signal intervention his complete stops increased to 31%. Then, during the individual-based turn-signal intervention, this deliverer's complete stopping decreased over 4 weeks, eventually reaching zero complete stopping. This downward trend during the individual-based turn-signal intervention is also seen in Drivers A-65 and B-71.

The deliverers whose complete stopping percentages are depicted in

FIGURE 36. Percent weekly complete stopping across baseline, group goal-setting and feedback intervention, public individualized feedback intervention, and follow-up phases for individuals during Ludwig, Geller, and Clarke (1999).

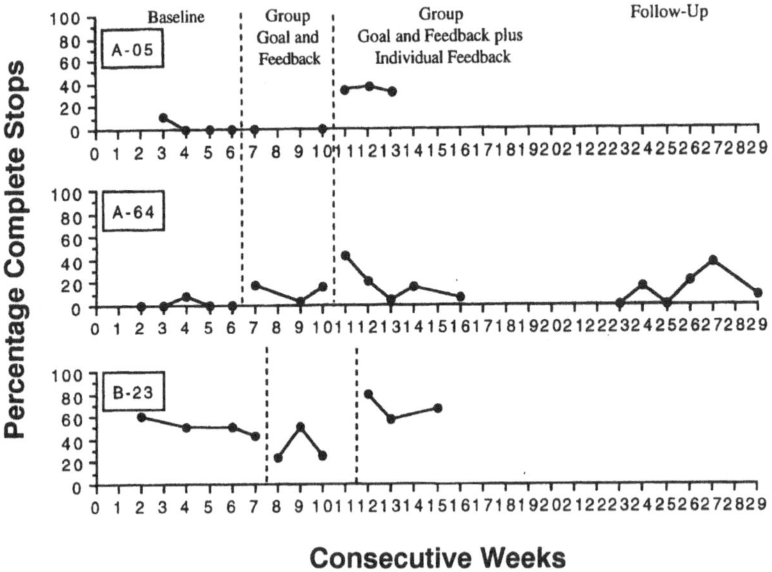

Figure 36 did not show an increase in complete stopping during the group intervention that targeted turn-signal use. However, they did show substantial increases in complete stopping during the individual intervention. Driver A-05 had almost 0% complete stopping during the baseline and group intervention phases but then jumped to 35% complete stopping throughout the individual intervention. Driver B-23's increase during the individual intervention was also maintained throughout the entire phase. Driver A-64's increase in complete stopping occurred only during the first week of the individual intervention then decreased back to baseline levels over the next two weeks. Like all the individual deliverers depicted in Figure 35, Drivers A-05 and A-64 only began to show an increase in turn-signal use during the individual intervention, not the group intervention.

The deliverers' driving data plotted in Figure 37 revealed an increasing trend in complete stopping over the two intervention phases. Driver A-94 came to a complete stop 0% of the time during baseline,

FIGURE 37. Percent weekly complete stopping across baseline, group goal-setting and feedback intervention, public individualized feedback intervention, and follow-up phases for individuals during Ludwig, Geller, and Clarke (1999).

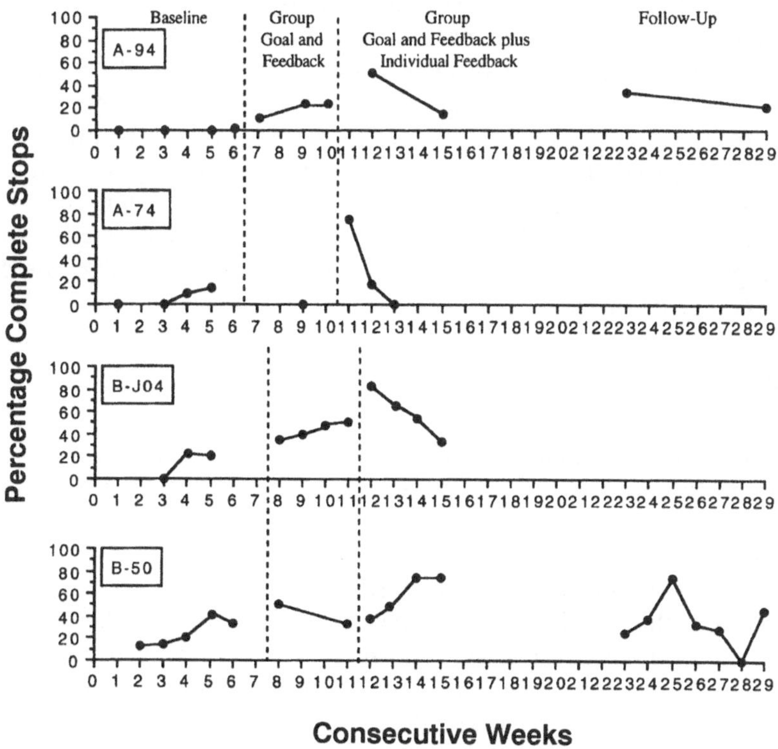

gradually increased to 21% during the group intervention, and had a rather high percentage of complete stops during one week of the individual intervention, followed by a drop to 18% four weeks later. Driver B-J04 had the same trend, nearly tripling his complete stopping during the individual intervention before reversing to baseline levels. Drivers A-74 and B-50 show similar and prominent increases in complete stops over the group and individual interventions. However, these two deliverers maintained their complete stopping during the intervention. Driver B-50 increased his complete stopping throughout the individual intervention, although he had an increasing trend during baseline.

In summary, we have used more than one approach to demonstrate response generalization. We have shown generalization among behaviors that were correlated in baseline and among behaviors uncorrelated in baseline. We have demonstrated response generalization across a variety of interventions both on the group-aggregate level and for individual drivers. We argue that the desirable effect of response generalization is a crucial index of intervention effectiveness. If, however, undesired behaviors are increased along with desirable changes in the targeted behavior(s), then not only is the effectiveness of the intervention compromised but its social validity is also in jeopardy. Therefore, it is important to determine whether the spread of an intervention's effect is desirable or undesirable, and to define factors that can increase generalization and decrease the undesirable spread of effect referred to as countercontrol.

Countercontrol

Applied behavior analysts have been accused of creating aversive situations for clients (Balsam & Bondy, 1983; Miller, 1991). Hung (1987) suggested that intervention programs can actually detract from reinforcing activities in the normal life of a person. Likewise, injury control interventions on the job sometimes require employees to make pronounced changes in the way they work, and often subject employees to compulsory training and monitoring. In response to this kind of external control, individuals may attempt countercontrol measures (Miller, 1991; Skinner, 1953).

Normally, countercontrol is referred to as an undesired change in a target behavior. Mawhinney and Fellows-Kubet (1999) present data showing two telemarketers responding to a token and lottery-based performance incentive intervention by substantially lowering their phone call productivity. Bensley and Wu (1991) report high-threat alcohol prevention messages actually resulted in males consuming more beer in a taste test than males who received low-threat messages.

Impact on Target Behavior. In our studies, we have seen numerous examples of individuals exhibiting countercontrol by decreasing their incidents of the targeted behavior. For example, in the Ludwig, Geller, and Clarke (1999) study, Driver B-03, (see Figure 38), decreased his turn-signal use from a baseline mean of 83% to a low of 25% toward the end of the individual intervention. Figure 3 presented data from an individual deliverer (i.e., D-007) from the Ludwig and Geller (1991)

FIGURE 38. Percent weekly turn-signal use across baseline, group goal-setting and feedback intervention, public individualized feedback intervention, and follow-up phases for Driver B-03 during Ludwig, Geller, and Clarke (1999).

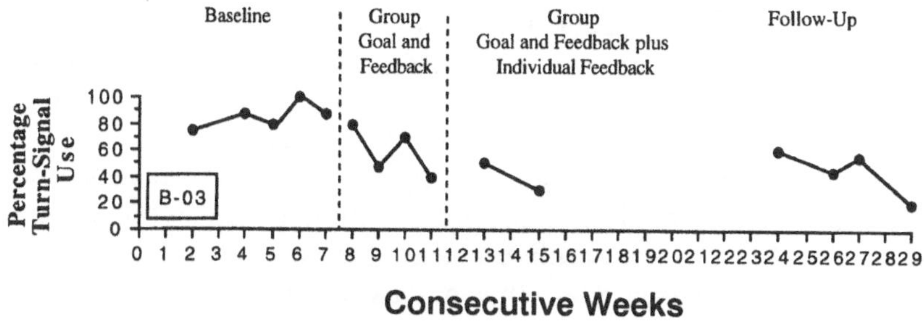

study who decreased his safety-belt use from 100% during Baseline to 0% during the intervention.

Impact on Non-Targeted Behaviors. Rarely has countercontrol been identified in behaviors not targeted by an intervention. However, organizations often deal with incidents of vandalism, theft, and absenteeism that may be associated with top-down attempts to control employee behavior. One of the authors, for example, witnessed an increase in tobacco stains on walls in a warehouse corresponding with the implementation of a strict production quota system. The target of the quota system was productivity, which the organization got. However, during this time there was more damage to product, more incorrect deliveries, and an increase in vandalism and theft.

Geller, Casali, and Johnson (1980) investigated the relationship between safety-belt use and the intrusiveness of safety-belt inducement devices including various light and buzzer reminders and the ignition interlock system. They found that as safety-belt inducement interventions became more intrusive and controlling, people were more likely to defeat the system by either sitting on a buckled safety belt or completely disconnecting the system. Overall, 42% had defeated their safety-belt inducement system. Similarly, Janssen (1994) found that when hard-core nonusers of safety-belts were forced to buckle-up, they drove faster, followed more closely behind vehicles in front of them, changed lanes at higher speeds, and braked later when approaching obstacles.

Two of our studies demonstrated countercontrol in non-targeted behaviors at the group-aggregate level. Ludwig and Geller (1999) reported a decrease in safety-belt use after deliverers received turn-signal policies. In another study, Ludwig and Geller (1997) reported a decrease in turn-signal use when deliverers were assigned a goal to increase their complete stopping at intersections (i.e., the assigned group). Using individual data from this group, we created arrow-enhanced scatterplots to show the relationship between the targeted complete stopping and the non-targeted behaviors of safety-belt and turn-signal use across the baseline and intervention phases.

Data plotted in Figure 39 graphically depict the correlations between these behaviors during the intervention phase overlaid with deliverers' data from the baseline phase. Arrows connect deliverers' data across these phases. Data that moves up and to the left on the scatterplot is indicative of instances when a deliverer's mean percentage of complete stopping during the intervention increased while their mean percentage of safety-belt or turn-signal use decreased. A pattern such as this is indicative of the phenomenon called countercontrol.

Individual Drivers

Even when the aggregate group data show desirable response generalization, individuals demonstrate countercontrol by decreasing their mean percentage of non-targeted behaviors. In the Ludwig, Geller, and Clarke (1999) study, the two experimental stores increased complete stops during the two turn-signal interventions. However, three deliverers, depicted in Figure 40, decreased their complete stopping as they increased their turn-signal use during the interventions. Driver B-69 began with a baseline mean of 49% complete intersection stops then decreased to 29% during the group intervention. Then he decreased further to 23% during the individual intervention.

Driver B-97 had the same pattern of decreasing complete intersection stops, from a baseline of 54% complete intersection stops to a group intervention mean of 29%, and then an individual intervention mean of 45%. Finally, Driver B-03 also had a decreasing trend, from 48% complete intersection stops during baseline, to 19% during the group intervention, and then to 21% during the individual intervention. However, Drivers B-97 and B-03 had already had a downward trend in the non-targeted behavior during baseline.

FIGURE 39. Scatterplots linking individual complete stopping and turn-signal or safety-belt use across baseline and intervention phases of Ludwig and Geller (1997). Filled circles represent data from selected deliverers during baseline. Open squares represent data from individual deliverers during the intervention phase. Arrows link selected deliverers' data across baseline and intervention phases.

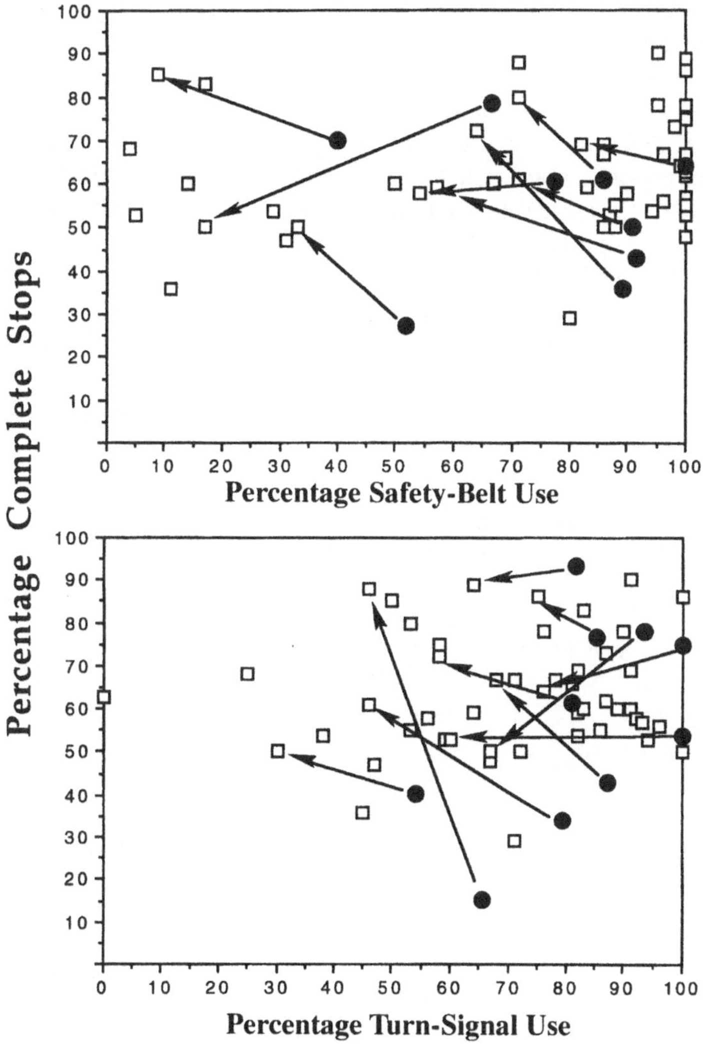

Risk Homeostasis

An alternative explanation for countercontrol as specifically applied to safety, is found in the theory of risk homeostasis (Wilde, 1982). Risk homeostasis theory purports that at any point in time, individuals perceive (and are willing to accept) a certain level of risk. When one's perceived and accepted levels of risk are not in equilibrium, the individual presumably alters his/her behavior in such a manner as to bring the perceived and accepted levels of risk into homeostatic balance. Thus, efforts to increase the frequency of one safe behavior may have the *undesirable* side-effect of decreasing other safe behaviors within the same response class. This implies that following an intervention that successfully increases a safe behavior (such as safety-belt use), an individual may perform a less safe behavior (such as increasing vehicle speed) in order to maintain a certain level of risk homeostasis.

Wilde reviewed traffic safety statistics and suggested overall crash rates return to baseline levels after the implementation of such safety

FIGURE 40. Percent weekly complete stopping across baseline, group goal-setting and feedback intervention, public individualized feedback intervention, and follow-up phases for individuals during Ludwig, Geller, and Clarke (1999).

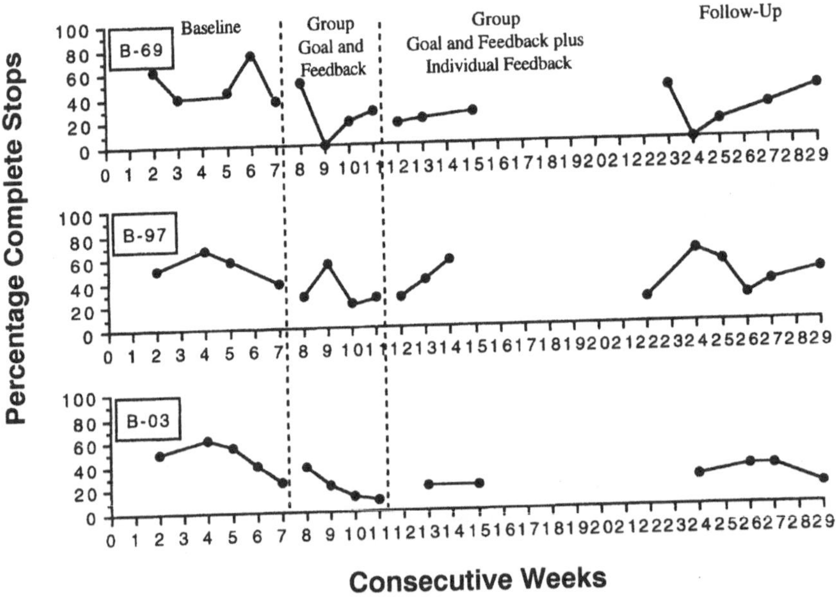

interventions as encouraging drivers to use their low beam lights instead of parking lights after dusk (Schreuder, 1969) or installing a three-phase traffic light (Short, Woelfl, & Change, 1982). In Australia, mandatory safety-belt use laws were associated with an immediate 12% reduction in road fatalities within the first two years. However, over the next six years road fatalities increased about 20% in comparison to no-law countries (Adams, 1981). Finally, in another domain, Lee (1979) reported that doctors who reduced their cigarette smoking were less likely to die from a smoking-related illness, but they were more likely to die from alcohol consumption, vehicle crashes, and other causes.

Although lending support to Wilde's theory, this evidence may be considered anecdotal in terms of showing actual behavior change, because it focused only on group outcome measures tracked over a number of years. Risk homeostatis, as it is described, is an individual phenomenon and cannot be supported with group statistics. One notable exception was a study by Streff and Geller (1988). These researchers found when subjects operated a 5-hp go-cart on a closed track without a safety belt (for 15 laps) and then buckled up (for 15 laps), they increased their driving speed over subjects who did not buckle up for the second 15 laps.

Otherwise, both community-based (McKenna, 1985; O'Neil, Lund & Ashton, 1985) and laboratory (Wilde, Claxton-Oldfield, & Platenius, 1985) studies have found little support for risk homeostatis theory. Therefore it is not surprising that Wilde's theory of risk homeostasis is not supported when applied to the present set of studies. On a number of occasions, interventions that increased a targeted safety behavior were associated with a concomitant *increase* in a non-targeted safety behavior. Risk homeostasis theory predicts a decrease in non-targeted behaviors in nearly every circumstance. In contrast, contercontrol is predicted to occur only when the intervention is associated with strong external controls. And, it was under these conditions that we observed less response generalization and more undesirable changes in non-targeted behaviors.

Conclusions Regarding Spread of Effect

Because we observed the same two or three driving behaviors in seven field studies, we were able to analyze the relationship between these behaviors and how they changed within various intervention formats. Table 5 is a matrix that reveals relationships between behaviors targeted by the interventions in terms of the direction of changes in non-targeted behaviors (i.e., increase, decrease, or no change).

In the two studies where safety-belt use was targeted by the intervention, increases in turn-signal use were observed. However, the reverse relationship was not evident. When turn-signal use was targeted by an intervention, there were no instances of safety-belt use increasing at the same time.

There is some evidence that safety-belt use does increase in the

TABLE 5. Changes in Targeted (in shaded boxes) and Nontargeted (in non-shaded boxes) Behaviors Across Studies

Studies: Intervention	Targeted Behavior	Direction of Behavior Change		
		Safety-Belt	Turn-Signal	Complete Stop
Ludwig & Geller (1991): Awareness and Promise Card	Safety-Belt Use	Increase	Increase	Not Observed
Ludwig & Geller (1999): Community		Increase	Increase	Not Observed
Ludwig & Geller (1999): Policy	Turn-Signal Use	Decrease	Small Increase	Not Observed
Ludwig, Geller, & Clarke (1999): Group and Individual Feedback		No change	Increase	Increase
Ludwig, Biggs, Wagner, & Geller (1999): Competition–Turn-Signal Target		No change	Increase	No Increase
Ludwig (1999): Static Goal		No change	Increase	Decrease
Ludwig (1999): Dynamic Goal		No change	No change	No change
Ludwig (1999): Static & Dynamic Goal		No change	Increase	Increase
Ludwig & Geller (1997): Participative Goals and Feedback	Complete Stops	Increase	Increase	Increase
Ludwig & Geller (1997): Assigned Goals and Feedback		No change	Decrease	Increase
Ludwig, Biggs, Wagner, & Geller (1999): Competition-Stops Targeted		Increase	No change	Increase

context of interventions targeting complete stopping. No consistent pattern emerged, however, when looking at relationships between turn-signal use and complete stopping. Whether turn-signal use increased during complete stopping interventions depended on the particular intervention. The same can be said for complete stopping increasing during interventions designed to increase the use of vehicle turn-signals.

What is evident across our studies is that the spread of an intervention's impact, whether in the form of response generalization or countercontrol, is a robust finding that can be replicated. Response generalization seems to increase as a function of employee involvement, whereas countercontrol seems to increase with top-down external consequences. Thus, we believe a spread-of-effect can occur, and certain conditions determine whether this side-effect is positive (generalization) or negative (countercontrol). But what mechanisms can explain such indirect effects of an intervention program?

Failure to Demonstrate Tight Control. If the operations of an intervention program in studies such as ours do not adequately differentiate a specific behavior, individuals may fail to discriminate between the target response and other behaviors. Thus, they might emit a variety of behaviors other than the target behavior. In fact, it is possible that changes in non-targeted behaviors during our interventions could be due to our failure to demonstrate tight control over all aspects of the antecedents and consequences offered in the intervention. Indeed, Stokes and Baer (1977) called for the use of "loose training" and "indiscriminable contingencies" in their suggestions regarding how to increase generalization across settings, subjects, trainers, time, and behaviors.

However, we consider generalization to be an *active* process instead of one that is *passive* and simply considered as a failure to control the critical variables sufficiently. As we progressed with our series of studies using pizza deliverers, we attempted to gain tighter control over our intervention process in order to differentiate the target behavior. In two studies (Ludwig & Geller, 1991, 1997) we had meetings with the managers and instructed them not to mention any other behaviors than complete stopping during the 4 weeks of the intervention. Afterwards the managers said they had complied. We videotaped the intervention meetings, and after independent viewings by observers "blind" to the study's aims, we determined that there were no references to turn-signal or safety-belt use. This videotaping procedure was also used in the Ludwig, Geller, and Clarke (1999) study.

Additionally, as we began to use individualized feedback as an intervention strategy, we had no personal contact with the deliverers, and we presented feedback posters, rewards (Ludwig, Biggs, Wagner, & Geller, 1999), or memos (Ludwig, 1999) that were specific to only the single behavior targeted by the intervention. As we "tightened" our intervention process to further differentiate the target behavior, we saw no decreases in the amount of response generalization.

Finally, a "loose training" explanation does not account for *decreases* in non-targeted behaviors during an intervention. The fact we were able to demonstrate both an increase and a decrease in non-targeted behaviors, depending on our intervention strategy, suggests that an explanation other than loose training is in order.

Previous Associations. Perhaps a more instructive way to approach response generalization and countercontrol is to consider prior associations between target and non-target behaviors. There are many reliable instances of associations made in the past that a population of individuals can share. In industrial settings, for example, extensive training programs associate many types of safety behaviors in the daily routine of the employee. For example, Fellner and Sulzer-Azaroff (1985) reported an industrial intervention that aggregated safety behaviors into "practices" and "conditions" groups. Behaviors such as putting on "ear protection," "turning equipment off when not in use," and "using guards when operating machinery" were grouped under the outcome of "safety practices." All the behaviors specified by Fellner and Sulzer-Azaroff under "safety practices" were associated during their intervention.

Similarly, the nationwide driver safety program implemented by one of the national pizza chains in 1990 taught deliverers to associate a number of diverse safe-driving behaviors, including: (a) driving within the posted speed limit, (b) coming to complete stops at all intersections, (c) remaining two car-lengths behind vehicles, (d) yielding to pedestrians, (e) using turn-signals and safety-belts, (f) keeping vehicles well maintained, and (g) practicing safe passing, merging, and backing up.

Such employee training programs are reliable sources of behavioral associations because all employees undergo the same training as part of their job. Likewise, it can be assumed that many safe driving behaviors have been associated for the general public as a result of participation in public driver education courses to earn licenses. Behavioral associations could even be created through training, policy enforcement procedures, social interactions, watching others, or actual involvement in vehicle wrecks. These associations shape a pattern of rule-governed behaviors that may be shared by many individuals in a given organization or community.

Rule-Governed Behavior. Response generalization exemplifies the complexity of human responding. Previous associations create rule-governed behaviors describing the correct actions to be taken in the context of an environmental event. Rules themselves are not discriminative stimuli (i.e., signaling the occasion when a certain response will be followed by a consequence). Instead, rules alter the function of other stimuli and designate them as discriminative stimuli (Blakely & Schlinger, 1987; Schlinger & Blakely, 1987).

A rule can specify a three-term contingency. What is important for our discussion is that a rule need not stipulate only a single behavior as part of the three-term contingency. Instead, when developed over an individual's lifetime of experiences with societal (including work-related) or environmental consequences, rules stipulate a number of similar behaviors that are functionally related to the three-term contingency.

Therefore, if members of a population all engage in common rule-governed behavior (based on common learning histories; Wanchisen & Tatham, 1991), then it is expected that all behaviors relevant to a rule (through previous associations) will correlate. Additionally, if an intervention targets one behavior that is associated with a rule, then other behaviors specified by that rule may also change. It is possible that many of our interventions activated rule-governed behaviors along with the targeted behavior.

In the context of our Behavior Change Taxonomy, we argue that interventions involving individuals can provide a context that promotes response generalization. Involvement and ownership in an intervention process can activate previously held rules and thus rule-governed behaviors. When individuals become committed to an intervention through involvement and ownership, they have an opportunity to verbalize their previously-held rules.

In a few of our studies (Ludwig & Geller, 1991, 1997; Ludwig, Geller, & Clarke, 1999), we asked deliverers why it is a good idea to engage in the targeted behavior. To answer this question they often referred to legal (i.e., tickets), social (being yelled at), or physical (damage to car or self) consequences. These same consequences pertain to driving safety behaviors other than those targeted by the intervention. Even though these other behaviors were not mentioned during the discussion, their relationship with these common verbalized consequences may have evoked rule-governed behavior in the context of the intervention.

Therefore, when interventions were high in involvement, targeting one behavior also activated a number of rule-governed behaviors as well, some of which we systematically observed. The high-involvement interventions reported in Ludwig and Geller (1991, 1997) and in Ludwig, Geller, and Clarke (1999) were all associated with response generalization.

In contrast, some of our interventions (Ludwig, Biggs, Wagner, & Geller, 1999; Ludwig & Geller, 1997) focused on external consequences such as assigned goals, managerial surveillance, or individual competition. In these cases, the target behavior was instrumental in attaining the direct external consequences. For example, deliverers were *following managerial mandates* (Ludwig & Geller, 1997, 1999a), or *competing for a reward* (Ludwig, Biggs, Wagner, & Geller, 1999). In these situations, no behavior other than the target behavior was reinforced by the external consequences. It is likely the deliverers in these studies were not engaging in the behavior for personal reasons associated with previously-established rules. As a result, rule-governed behavior associated with other safe driving behaviors was not activated. Response generalization is unlikely to occur under these circumstances because non-targeted behaviors within "safe driving/avoid injury" rules would not be activated by the external consequences.

The circumstantial limitations of response generalization are understandable in the context of the pizza delivery business. Assuming individual driving behavior was rule governed before being employed, pizza deliverers were required to incorporate new behaviors in their capacity as a pizza deliverer. For example, from the start, they were taught to review a map before beginning their trip, run to their car, and keep their car running when going to a customer's door. It is doubtful the deliverers engaged in these behaviors previously or, for that matter, while driving during their free time. These behaviors are obviously associated with rules specific to their job. We suggest that when an intervention offers rules specific to the job, as mandated by the manager or by external "top-down" contingencies, then the behavior is governed by job-specific contingencies.

In summary, the Behavior Change Taxonomy suggests that response generalization will be less likely to occur during interventions with strong external consequences and minimal employee involvement. In fact, when our interventions were more controlling such as the assigned-goals group in Ludwig and Geller (1997) and during the competition in Ludwig, Biggs, Wagner and Geller (1999) no increases were seen in the non-targeted behaviors of turn-signal use or complete stopping.

OVERALL CONCLUSIONS

Motor vehicle wrecks are a prominent cause of injury and death for large numbers of employees for whom driving is a primary aspect of their occupation. As the demand for delivery of products and services grows, so will the number of driving-related occupations. Therefore, safety leaders within industry and government need more effective and predictable tools to promote safe driving among these growing numbers of individuals. This monograph described two models developed to help intervention agents choose more effective behavior change techniques when planning their safety programs.

The MIL Model

The Multiple Intervention Level (MIL) model suggests that more intrusive interventions are required to change the behavior of individuals who are not affected by large-scale interventions. Among the interventions evaluated in this monograph, a few were not very intrusive. For example, the awareness and promise-card intervention (Ludwig & Geller, 1991), the community program (Ludwig & Geller, 1999b), and the policy intervention (1999a) were all group-level interventions. Likewise, the group goal-setting and feedback interventions (Ludwig & Geller, 1997; Ludwig, Geller, & Clarke, 1999) did not single out employees for personal antecedents (i.e., goals) or consequences (i.e., feedback).

These group-level interventions can be contrasted with the interventions that provided deliverers with individualized feedback (Ludwig, Geller, & Clarke, 1999; Ludwig, Biggs, Wagner, & Geller, 1999) and, in one case, individualized goal setting (Ludwig, 1999). The MIL model proposes that these individualized interventions are necessary for those individuals unaffected by the less intrusive group-level interventions. In fact, in studies where individualized feedback was provided, we saw more individuals comply with the intervention and increase the targeted behavior.

The Ludwig, Geller, and Clarke (1999) study exemplifies how a group-level intervention can fail to influence some deliverers. However, when the individualized feedback was introduced, the very individuals who did not comply with the group intervention had the most improvement. It was also interesting that the individuals who were affected by the initial group-level intervention did not, for the most part, show continued increases during the individualized intervention.

On the basis of our findings, intervention agents planning an intervention to improve safety-related behaviors should begin with a large-scale program targeting all their employees with group meetings, sign-based prompts, and other uses of media. Subsequently, they should enroll those employees who were influenced by the first intervention to become agents of change for the more intrusive interventions needed for those "holdouts" uninfluenced by the less intrusive techniques. In this manner, intervention planners can increase the agent-to-participant ratio and, at the same time, continue to influence the behavior of those agents they enrolled, as seen in the Ludwig and Geller (1999b) community program.

The Behavior Change Taxonomy

The Behavior Change Taxonomy offers a comprehensive look at intervention effectiveness. Intervention impact refers to not only behavior change concurrent with the intervention but also the maintained impact after the intervention is withdrawn. In addition, the impact on behaviors not directly targeted by an intervention is considered. Although many more direct empirical tests of hypotheses generated from this model are needed, including those that measure intervening factors such as involvement and peer support more directly, we can draw some tentative conclusions from the studies reviewed in this monograph.

Table 6 summarizes the results of seven studies into concurrent impact, maintained impact, and spread-of-effect (response generalization or countercontrol). This table also scores each intervention on Involvement, Peer Support, Response Information, and External Control. In addition, each intervention is broken down into the behavior change techniques from the taxonomy (see Table 1) that were used to derive the scoring.

For example, an intervention such as the individualized feedback with competitive rewards (Ludwig, Biggs, Wagner, & Geller, 1999) uses the following techniques: (a) Written Activators, (b) Individual Feedback, and (c) Individual Competition. Each of these techniques has been assigned a taxonomy score of a "1" or a "0" for each of the taxonomy factors (i.e., Involvement, Peer Support, Response Information, and External Contingencies) depending on whether the technique uses these factors or not. Adding the "1"s and "0"s of the three techniques for each factor gives this particular intervention a "1" for Involvement, "0" for Peer Support, "3" for Response Information, and "2" for External Contingencies.

Cross-study comparisons are difficult because of different target behaviors and baseline levels. Additionally, our samples were not equivalent across studies because we used different stores in different towns and states. Finally, these studies took place over a long period of time, and as such, various local safety efforts by companies (such as the driver safety program) or states (e.g., Buckle-Up laws) influenced baseline levels of observed behaviors. And, the impact of our interventions were likely affected by these various contextual events. Nevertheless, certain consistent patterns did emerge.

Interventions that received a score for all four factors (Involvement, Peer Support, Response Information, and External Contingencies) seemed to have the greatest *concurrent impact,* especially those with higher scores. It was also advantageous to have a low baseline. This was often the effect found when many techniques were used to comprise the intervention and when there were high levels of Response Information. Response Information was highest in interventions offering individualized feedback (i.e., Ludwig, 1999; Ludwig, Biggs, Wagner, & Geller, 1999; Ludwig, Geller, & Clarke, 1999).

Interventions associated with greater *maintained effects* were higher in Involvement and Peer Support and had lower amounts of External Contingencies. The awareness and promise-card intervention (Ludwig &

TABLE 6. The Results of the Seven Studies Reviewed in This Monograph in the Context of the Behavior Change Taxonomy. "Belts" Refers to Safety-Belt Use. "Signals" Refers to Turn-Signal Use. "Stops" Refers to Complete Intersection Stops

Study Description			Taxonomy Factor Scores							Spread of Effect		
Intervention (Study) Taxonomy Techniques Stores	Targeted Behavior	Baseline Behavior	Involvement	Peer Support	Response Information	External Control	Concurrent Effects	Maintained Effects	Non-Targeted Behavior	Baseline	Intervention	Withdrawl/ Follow-Up
Awareness Program (Ludwig & Geller, 1991) 4,5,7,8	Safety Belts		2	2	4	0						
Store A		41%					68%	69%	Signals	58%	74%	65%
Store B		14%					69%	41%	Signals	40%	49%	45%
Policy (Ludwig & Geller, 1999) 3,7	Turn Signals		0	0	2	1					Policy #1	Policy #2
Store A		70%					78%	84%	Belts	78%	65%	79%
Store B		46%					51%	59%	Belts	74%	59%	70%
Group Goal Setting and Feedback (Ludwig & Geller, 1997)	Complete Stops											
Participative Group 5,7,20,24		54%	2	3	4	1	66%	60/53%	Belts Signals	75% 68%	85% 76%	84/88% 78/72%
Assigned Group 1,7,19,24		45%	0	2	4	2	69%	59/42%	Belts Signals	57% 66%	56% 62%	58/61% 53/51%
Group and Individualized Feedback (Ludwig, Geller, & Clarke, 1999)	Turn Signals											
Group Goals & Feedback 5,7,20,24 Store A Store B		6% → 33%	2	3	4	1	21% 53%		Stops Stops	12% 30%	16% 35%	
Add Individualized Fdbk. 5,7,15,20,24 Store A Store B			2	3	5	2	↓ 32% → 59%	21% 36%	Stops Stops		↓ 18% 48%	21% 36%
Individualized Feedback and Competition (Ludwig, Biggs, Wagner, & Geller, 1999) 7,11,14,15			0	0	4	3						
Store A	Turn Signals	35%					58%	53%	Belts Stops	59% 35%	73% 29%	86% 49%
Store B	Stops	14%					31%	21%	Belts Signals	64% 25%	57% 29%	52% 12%
Dynamic and Static Goals (Ludwig, 1999) 7,9,14	Turn Signals		0	0	3	2						
Dynamic		42%					58%	53%	Belts Stops	66% 45%	64% 34%	68% 38%
Static		47%					49%	57%	Belts Stops	82% 38%	85% 39%	78% 42%
Dynamic/Static		42%					70%	44%	Belts Stops	76% 39%	78% 47%	74% 39%
Community Program (Ludwig & Geller, 1999) 6,7,8	Safety Belts		1	2	3	0						
Store A		57%					75%	74%	Signals	54%	76%	73%

Geller, 1991), community program (Ludwig & Geller, 1999b), and the participative goal-setting and feedback intervention (Ludwig & Geller, 1997) are good examples of this. We believe Involvement and Peer Support are techniques that result in safety antecedents and consequences becoming more indigenously supported and thereby are more likely to be sustained by the culture after the intervention is discontinued. In contrast, the impact of techniques that are high in External Contingencies are more likely to cease when these more contrived, less indigenous interventions are removed.

Finally, the amount of response generalization (a desirable spread-of-effect) seems related to the amount of Involvement offered by the intervention. This was seen in the results of the awareness and promise-card intervention in Ludwig and Geller (1991), the community program in Ludwig and Geller (1999b), the participation intervention in Ludwig and Geller (1997), and during the group-based intervention in Ludwig, Geller, and Clarke (1999). In contrast, prominent amounts of External Contingencies in an intervention were often associated with instances of countercontrol (an undesirable spread of effect). The policy intervention in Ludwig and Geller (1999a), the assigned goal-setting intervention in Ludwig and Geller (1997), and the competition intervention in Ludwig, Biggs, Wagner, and Geller (1999) all scored high in External Contingencies and led to decreases in non-targeted safety-related behaviors during the intervention period.

Ultimately we hope to develop the Behavior Change Taxonomy into a practical tool for intervention planners who wish to maximize both long-term and generalized impact. At this point, our research indicates that the most beneficial behavior-change interventions should offer opportunities for involvement, foster peer support, and provide dynamic response information. Interventions using external contingency procedures need to be developed with substantial employee involvement in order to avoid countercontrol or undesirable influence on non-targeted behaviors.

This research did not go so far as to offer confirmatory hypothesis testing of our models. Instead, the results are intended to demonstrate the efficacy of certain intervention techniques in improving the lives of occupational drivers by helping them avoid unnecessary injury and death. We hope the presentation of these models and our studies in this monograph will inspire more rigorous tests of the predictions made in these models. More importantly, we look forward to more relevant large-scale application and evaluation of the intervention techniques prescribed by these models.

AUTHOR NOTE

The authors acknowledge the significant contribution of research associates with the Center for Organization and Health Behavior at Appalachian State University and the Center for Applied Behavior Systems at Virginia Tech. Preparation of this report was supported in part by Grant Number 1 R01 OHMH03397-01 from the National Institute for Occupational Safety and Health (NIOSH), Centers for Disease Control and Prevention.

REFERENCES

Adams, J. (1981; as cited in Wilde, 1982). *The efficacy of seat belt legislation: A comparative study of road accident fatality statistics from 18 countries.* London, UK: University College.

Alavosius, M. P., & Sulzer-Azaroff, B. (1986). The effects of performance feedback on the safety of client lifting and transfer. *Journal of Applied Behavior Analysis, 19,* 261-267.

Allison, D. B., Silverstein, J. M., & Galante, V. (1992). Relative effectiveness and cost-effectiveness of cooperative, competitive, and independent monetary incentive systems. *Journal of Organizational Behavior Management, 13,* 85-112.

Baer, D. M., Wolf, M. M., & Risley, T. R. (1968). Some current dimensions of applied behavior analysis. *Journal of Applied Behavior Analysis, 1,* 91-97.

Balcazar, F., Hopkins, B. L., & Suarez, Y. (1986). A critical, objective review of performance feedback. *Journal of Organizational Behavior Management, 7,* 65-89.

Balsam, P. D., & Bondy, A. S. (1983). The negative side effects of reinforcement. *Journal of Applied Behavior Analysis, 16,* 283-296.

Bandura, A. (1969). *Principles of behavior modification.* New York: Holt, Rinehart & Winston.

Bandura, A., & Schunk, D. H. (1981). Cultivating competence, self-efficacy, and intrinsic interest through proximal self-motivation. *Journal of Personality and Social Psychology, 41,* 586-598.

Bandura, A., & Simon, K. M. (1977). The role of proximal intentions in self-regulation of refractory behavior. *Cognitive Therapy and Research, 1,* 177-193.

Baum, W. M. (1994). Modern perspectives on John B. Watson and classical behaviorism. *Contributions in Psychology, 24,* 133-140.

Bensley, L. S., & Wu, R. (1991). The role of psychological reactance in drinking following alcohol prevention messages. *Journal of Applied Social Psychology, 21,* 1111-1124.

Bijou, S. W., & Baer, D. M. (1961). *Child development. Vol. 1. A systematic and empirical theory.* New York: Appleton-Century-Crofts.

Blakely, E., & Schlinger, H. (1987). Rules: Function-altering contingency-specifying stimuli. *Behavior Analyst, 10,* 183-187.

Burleigh, R. A., & Marholin, D. (1977). Don't shoot until you see the whites of his eyes: An analysis of the adverse side effects of verbal prompts. *Behavior Modification, 1,* 109-122.

Campbell, R. J., Hunter, W. W., & Stutts, J. C. (1984). The use of economic incentives and education to modify safety-belt use behavior of high school students. *Health Education, 15,* 30-33.

Campbell, B. J., Stewart, J. R., & Campbell, F. A. (1987). *1985-1986 experiences with belt laws in the United States.* Chapel Hill, NC: UNC Highway Safety Research Center.

Carr, E. G. (1988). Functional equivalence as a mechanism of response generalization. In R. H. Horner, G. Dunlap, & R. L. Koegel (Eds.), *Generalization and maintenance* (pp. 221-241). Baltimore: Paul H. Brooks.

Catania, A. C. (1979). *Learning.* Englewood Cliffs, NJ: Prentice-Hall.

Cerutti, D. T. (1989). Discrimination theory and rule-governed behavior. *Journal of the Experimental Analysis of Behavior, 51,* 259-276.

Cervone, D. (1989). Effects of envisioning future activities on self-efficacy judgments and motivation: An availability heuristic interpretation. *Cognitive Therapy and Research, 13,* 247-261.

Cervone, D., & Peake, P. K. (1986). Anchoring efficacy, and action: The influence of judgmental heuristics on self-efficacy judgments and behavior. *Journal of Personality and Social Psychology, 50,* 492-501.

Clayton, M. C., Mawhinney, T. C., Luke, D. E., & Cook, H. G. (1997). Improving the management of overtime costs through decentralized controls: Managing an organizational metacontingency. *Journal of Organizational Behavior Management, 17,* 77-98.

Coleman, R. (1974). Response generalization in two catagories of classroom behavior. *Psychological Reports, 34,* 1167-1173.

Cooper, M. D., Phillips, R. A., Sutherland, V. J., & Makin, P. J. (1994). Reducing accidents using goal setting and feedback: A field study. *Journal of Occupational and Organizational Psychology, 67,* 219-240.

Cope, J. G., & Geller, E. S. (1984). Community-based interventions to increase the use of automobile litter bags. *Journal of Resource Management and Technology, 13,* 127-132.

Cope, J. G., Smith, G. A., & Grossnickle, W. F. (1986). The effect of variable rate cash incentives on safety-belt use. *Journal of Safety Research, 17,* 95-99.

Cravin, D. R. (1998). Domino's looks abroad to deliver more growth. *Crains' Detroit Business, 14,* pg. 3.

Domino's Pizza (1989). *Safe delivery program.* Ann Arbor, MI: Domino's Pizza, Inc.

Dubbert, P. M., & Wilson, G. T. (1984). Goal setting and spouse involvement in the treatment of obesity. *Behavior Research Therapy, 22,* 227-242.

Eisenberg, L. (1972). The human nature of human nature. *Science, 176,* 123-128.

Elman, D., & Killebrew, T. J. (1978). Incentives and seat belts: Changing a resistant behavior through extrinsic motivation. *Journal of Applied Social Psychology, 8,* 72-83.

Emmert, G. D. (1978). Measuring the impact of group performance feedback versus individual performance feedback in an industrial setting. *Journal of Organizational Behavior Management, 1,* 134-141.

Erez, M. (1977). Feedback: A necessary condition for the goal setting-performance relationship. *Journal of Applied Psychology, 62,* 624-627.

Erez, M. (1986). The congruence of goal setting strategies with socio-cultural values, and its effect on performance. *Journal of Management, 12,* 585-592.

Erez, M., & Arad, R. (1986). Participative goal setting: Social, motivational and cognitive factors. *Journal of Applied Psychology, 71,* 591-597.

Evans, L. (1985). Human behavior feedback and traffic safety. *Human Factors, 27,* 555-576.

Evans, L. (1991). *Traffic safety and the driver.* New York: Van Nostrand Reinhold.

Evans, L, Wasielewski, P., & von Buseck, C. R. (1982). Compulsory seat belt usage and driver risk-taking behavior. *Human Factors, 24,* 41-48.

Fellner, D. J., & Sulzer-Azaroff, B. (1984). Increasing industrial safety practices and conditions through posted feedback. *Journal of Safety Research, 15,* 7-21.

Fellner, D. J., & Sulzer-Azaroff, B. (1985). Occupational safety: Assessing the impact of adding assigned or participative goal setting. *Journal of Organizational Behavior Management, 7,* 3-24.

Ferguson, B., & Blampied, N. M. (1991). Unenlightened: An unsuccessful attempt to promote the use of cycle lights at night. *Accident Analysis and Prevention, 23,* 561-571.

Festinger, L. (1957). A theory of cognitive dissonance. New York: Harper and Row.

Fredda, J. V., & Ludwig, T. D. (1999). *The effects of proximal and distal goal setting on academic performance.* Unpublished manuscript, Appalachian State University, Boone, NC.

Geller, E. S. (1983). Rewarding safety-belt usage at an industrial setting: Tests of treatment generality and response maintenance. *Journal of Applied Behavior Analysis, 16,* 189-202.

Geller, E. S. (1984). Motivating safety belt use with incentives: A critical review of the past and a look to the future. *SAE Technical Paper Series* (No. 840326). Warrendale, PA: Society of Automotive Engineers.

Geller, E. S. (1987). Environmental psychology and applied behavior analysis: From strange bedfellows to a productive marriage. In D. Stokols and I. Altman (Eds.), *Handbook of environmental psychology,* Vol. 1 (pp. 361-338). New York: John Wiley & Sons.

Geller, E. S. (1988). A behavioral science approach to transportation safety. *Bulletin of the New York Academy of Medicine, 65,* 632-661.

Geller, E. S. (1990). Preventing injuries and deaths from vehicle crashes: Encouraging belts and discouraging booze. In J. Edwards, R.S. Tindale, L. Heath, & E. Posavac (Eds.), *Social influence processes and prevention.* New York: Plenum Press.

Geller, E. S. (1991a). If only more would actively care. *Journal of Applied Behavior Analysis, 24,* 601-612.

Geller, E. S. (1991b). Where's the validity in social validity? *Journal of Applied Behavior Analysis, 24,* 179-184.

Geller, E. S. (1994). The failure of safety goals. *Industrial Safety and Hygiene News, 28*(9), 13-14.

Geller, E. S. (1996). *The psychology of safety: How to change behaviors and attitudes on the job.* Radnor, PA: Chilton Book Company.

Geller, E. S. (1997). The three keys to safety success. *Industrial Safety and Hygiene News, 31*(5), 16-19.

Geller, E. S. (1998a). *Applications of behavior analysis to prevent injuries from vehicle crashes* (Second Edition). Cambridge, MA: Cambridge Center for Behavioral Studies.

Geller, E. S. (1998b). *Understanding behavior-based safety: Step-by-step methods to improve your workplace* (2nd Edition). Neenah, WI: J.J. Keller & Associates.

Geller, E. S., Berry, T.D., Ludwig, T.D., Evans, R.E., Gilmore, M.R., & Clarke, S.W. (1990). A conceptual framework for developing and evaluating behavior change interventions for injury control. *Health Education Research: Theory and Practice, 5*(2), 125-137.

Geller, E. S., Casali, J. G., & Johnson, R. P. (1980). Seat belt usage: A potential target for applied behavior analysts. *Journal of Applied Behavior Analysis, 13,* 669-675.

Geller, E. S., Johnson, R. P., & Pelton, S. L. (1982). Community-based interventions for encouraging safety-belt use. *American Journal of Community Psychology, 10,* 183-195.

Geller, E. S., & Kalsher, M. J. (1990). Environmental determinants of party drinking: Bartenders vs. self-service. *Environment and Behavior, 22,* 74-90.

Geller, E. S., Kalsher, M. S., Rudd, J. R., & Lehman, G. R. (1989). Promoting safety-belt use on a university campus: An integration of commitment and incentive strategies. *Journal of Applied Social Psychology, 19,* 3-19.

Geller, E. S., & Lehman, G. R. (1991). The buckle-up promise card: A versatile intervention for large-scale behavior change. *Journal of Applied Behavior Analysis, 24,* 91-94.

Geller, E. S., & Ludwig, T. D. (1991). A behavior change taxonomy for improving road safety. In M.J. Koornstra & J. Christensen (Eds.), *Enforcement and rewarding: Strategies and effects,* pp. 41-45. Proceedings of the OECD International Road Safety Conference, Copenhagen, Denmark.

Geller, E. S., Ludwig, T. D., Gilmore, M. R., & Berry, T. D. (1990). A taxonomy of behavior change: Techniques for community intervention. *The Community Psychologist, 23* (2), 4-6.

Geller, E. S., Needleman, L. D., & Randall, K. (1990). *Developing a taxonomy of behavior change techniques for environmental protection.* First U.S. Conference on Municipal Solid Waste Management, Washington, D.C.

Geller, E. S., Paterson, L., & Talbott, E. (1982). A behavioral analysis of incentive prompts for motivating seat belt usage. *Journal of Applied Behavior Analysis, 15,* 403-415.

Geller, E. S., Rudd, J. R., Kalsher, M. J., Streff, F. M., & Lehman, G. R. (1987). Employer-based programs to motivate safety-belt use: A review of short and long-term effects. *Journal of Safety Research, 18,* 1-17.

Geller, E. S., Winett, R. A., & Everett, P. B. (1982). *Preserving the environment: New strategies for behavior change.* Elmsford, New York: Pergamon Press.

Gollob, H. F., & Reichardt, C. S. (1991). Interpreting and estimating indirect effects assuming times lags really matter. In L. M. Collins & J. L. Horn (Eds.), *Best methods for the analysis of change: Recent advances, unanswered questions, future directions.* Washington, D.C.: American Psychological Association.

Grant, B. A. (1990). Effectiveness of feedback and education in an employment-based seat belt program. *Health Education Research, 5,* 2.

Greene, B. F., Winett, R. A., Van Houten, R., Geller, E. S., & Iwata, B. A. (Eds.). (1987). *Behavior analysis in the community: Readings from the Journal of Applied Behavior Analysis.* Lawrence, KS: University of Kansas Press.

Hall, H. K., & Byrne, A. T. (1988). Goal setting in sport: Clarifying recent anomalies. *Journal of Sport and Exercise Psychology, 10,* 184-198.

Hall, H. K., Weinberg, R. S., & Jackson, A. (1987). Effects of goal specificity, goal difficulty, and information feedback on endurance performance. *Journal of Sport Psychology, 9,* 43-54.

Hedlund, J. (1986, October). Casualty reductions: Results from safety-belt use laws. In *effectiveness of safety-belt use laws: A multinational examination.* US DOT, NHTSA, Report Number DOT HS 807 01118.

Hung, D. W. (1987). A matter of Self-reinforcing? *ABA Newsletter, 10,* 13-14.

Janssen, W. (1994). Seat-belt wearing and driving behavior: An instrumented-vehicle study. *Accident Analysis and Prevention, 26,* 249-261.

Jessor, R. (1987). Risky driving and adolescent problem behavior: An extension of problem behavior theory. *Alcohol, Drugs and Driving, 3,* 1-11.

Johnson, R. P., & Geller, E. S. (1980). Community mental health center programs. In D. Glenwick & L. Jason (Eds.), *Behavioral community psychology: Progress and prospects* (pp. 147-174). New York: Praeger Press.

Jones, R. T., Ollendick, T. H., McLaughlin, K. J., & Williams, C. E. (1989). Elaborative and behavioral reversal in the acquisition of fire emergency skills and the reduction of fear of fire. *Behavior Therapy, 20,* 93-101.

Kalsher, M. S., Geller, E. S., Clarke, S. W., & Lehman, G. R. (1989). Safety-belt promotion on a naval base: A comparison of incentives vs. disincentives. *Journal of Safety Research, 20,* 103-113.

Katz, E., & Lazarfeld, P. E. (1955). *Personal influence: The part played by people in the flow of mass communication.* Glencoe, IL: Free Press.

Kazdin, A. E. (1973). Methodological and assessment considerations in evaluating reinforcement programs in applied settings. *Journal of Applied Behavior Analysis, 6,* 517-531.

Kazdin, A. E. (1982). System substitution, generalization, and response covariation: Implications for psychotherapy outcome. *Psychological Bulletin, 91,* 349-365.

Keller, F. S. (1968). Good-bye teacher. . . . *Journal of Applied Behavior Analysis, 1,* 79-89.

Kello, J. E., Geller, E. S., Rice, J. C., & Bryant, S. L. (1988). Motivating auto safety belt wearing in industrial settings: From awareness to behavior change. *Journal of Organizational Behavior Management, 9,* 7-21.

Kernan, M. G., & Lord, R. G. (1988). Effects of participative vs. assigned goals and feedback in a multi-trial task. *Motivation and Emotion, 12,* 75-86.

Kirschenbaum, D. S. (1985). Proximity and specificity of planning: A position paper. *Cognitive Therapy and Research, 9,* 489-506.

Kirschenbaum, D. S., Humphrey, L. L., & Malett, S. D. (1981). Specificity of planning in adult self-control: An applied investigation. *Journal of Personality and Social Psychology, 40,* 941-950.

Kirschenbaum, D. S., Malett, S. D., Humphrey, L. L., & Tomarken, A. J. (1982). Specificity of planning and the maintenance of self-control: 1 year follow-up of a study improvement program. *Behavior Therapy, 13,* 232-240.

Komaki, J., Barwick, K. D., & Scott, L. R. (1978). A behavioral approach to occupational safety: Pinpointing and reinforcing safe performance in a food manufacturing plant. *Journal of Applied Psychology, 63,* 434-445.

Komaki, J., Collins, R. L., & Penn, P. (1982). The role of performance antecedents and consequences in work motivation. *Journal of Applied Psychology, 67,* 334-340.

Komaki, J., Heinemann, A. T., & Lawson, L. (1980). Effect of training and feedback: Component analysis of a behavioral safety program. *Journal of Applied Psychology, 65,* 261-270.

Kortick, S. A., & O'Brien, R. M. (1996). The world series of quality control: A case study in the package delivery industry. *Journal of Organizational Behavior Management, 16,* 77-93.

Larson, L. D., Schnelle, J. F., Kirchner, Jr., R., Carr, A. F., Domash, M, & Risley, T. R. (1980). Reduction of police vehicle accidents through mechanically aided supervision. *Journal of Applied Behavior Analysis, 13,* 571-581.

Latane, B., Williams, K., & Hawkins, S. (1979). *The unresponsive bystander: Why doesn't he help?* New York: Appleton-Century-Crofts.

Latham, G. P., Erez, M., & Locke, E. A. (1988). Resolving scientific disputes by the joint design of crucial experiments by the antagonists: Application to the Erez-Latham dispute regarding participation in goal setting. *Journal of Applied Psychology (Monograph), 73,* 753-772.

Latham, G. P., & Saari, L. M. (1979a). The effects of holding goal difficulty constant on assigned and participatory set goals. *Academy of Management Journal, 22,* 163-168.

Latham, G. P., & Saari, L. M. (1979b). Importance of supportive relationships in goal setting. *Journal of Applied Psychology, 64,* 151-156.

Latham, G. P., Steele, T. P., & Saari, L. M. (1982). The effects of participation and goal difficulty on performance. *Personnel Psychology, 35,* 677-686.

Latham, G. P., & Winters, D. W. (1989; as cited in Locke & Latham, 1990). *Separating the cognitive and motivational effects of participation on performance.* Unpublished manuscript, University of Washington, Seattle WA.

Lee, P. N. (1979). Has the morality of male doctors improved with the reduction in their cigarette smoking? *British Medical Journal, 2,* 1538-1540.

Locke, E. A., & Latham, G. P. (1990). *A theory of goal setting and task performance.* Englewood Cliffs, NJ: Prentice-Hall.

Ludwig, T. D. (1999). *Systematic treatments of goal-setting and feedback to increase safe driving among pizza deliverers.* Invited address for the Organizational Behavior Management Network Meeting, Daytona, FL.

Ludwig, T. D., Biggs, J., Wagner, S., & Geller, E. S. (1999). Using public feedback and competitive rewards to increase the safe driving of pizza deliverers. *Journal of Organizational Management* (in press).

Ludwig, T. D., & Geller, E. S. (1991). Improving the driving practices of pizza deliverers: Response generalization and moderating effects of driving history. *Journal of Applied Behavior Analysis, 24,* 31-34.

Ludwig, T. D., & Geller, E. S. (1997). Managing injury control among professional pizza deliverers: Effects of goal setting and response generalization. *Journal of Applied Psychology, 82,* 253-261.

Ludwig, T. D., & Geller, E. S. (1999a). Behavioral impact of a corporate driving policy: Undesirable side-effects reflect countercontrol. *Journal of Organizational Behavior Management, 19*(2), 25-34.

Ludwig, T. D., & Geller, E. S. (1999b). Behavior change among agents of a community safety program: Pizza deliverers advocate community safety belt use. *Journal of Organizational Behavior Management, 19*(2), 3-24.

Ludwig, T. D., Geller, E. S., & Clarke, S. W. (1999). Using publicly-displayed feedback to increase turn-signal use: Examining spread of effect to safe stops and safety-belt use. *Journal of Applied Behavior Analysis,* under review.

Malott, R. W. (1992). A theory of rule-governed behavior and organizational behavior management. *Journal of Organizational Behavior Management, 12*(2), 45-65.

Martens, B. K., & Witt, J. C. (1984). Assessment and prediction in an ecological system: Application of the general linear model of the response-class concept. *Journal of Behavioral Assessment, 6,* 197-206.

Martin, G., & Pear, J. (1996). *Behavior modification: What it is and how to do it* (Fifth Edition). Upper Saddle River, NJ: Prentice Hall.

Mawhinney, T. C., & Fellows-Kubert (1999). Positive contingencies versus quotas: Telemarketers exert countercontrol. *Journal of Organizational Behavior Management*, 19(2), 35-58.

McGinnis, J. M. (1984). Occupant protection as a priority in national efforts to promote health. *Health Education Quarterly, 11,* 127-131.

McKenna, F. P. (1985). Do safety measures really work? An examination of risk homeostasis theory. *Ergonomics, 28,* 489-498.

McLeskey, J., Rieth, H. J., & Polsgrove, L. (1980). The implications of response generalization for improving the effectiveness of programs for learning disabled children. *Journal of Learning Disabilities, 13,* 287-290.

Meagher, M. (1989, February). Death in the delivery zone (television segment). *Inside Edition,* American Broadcasting Company.

Melton, G. E. (1988). Adolescents and prevention of AIDS. *Professional Psychology: Research and Applications, 19(*4), 403-408.

Mento, A. J., Steel, R. P., & Karren, R. J. (1987). A meta-analytic study of the effects of goal setting on task performance: 1966-1984. *Organizational Behavior and Human Decision Processes, 39,* 52-83.

Michael, J. (1982). Distinguishing between discriminative and motivational functions of stimuli. *Journal of the Experimental Analysis of Behavior, 37,* 149-155.

Miller, L. K. (1991). Avoiding the countercontrol of applied behavior analysis. *Journal of Applied Behavior Analysis, 24,* 645-647.

Mischel, W., & Patterson, C. J. (1976). Substantive and structural elements of effective plans for self-control. *Journal of Personality and Social Psychology, 34,* 942-950.

Morgan, M. (1985). Self-monitoring of attained subgoals in private study. *Journal of Educational Psychology, 77,* 623-630.

National Center for Health Statistics (1999). *Healthy People 2000 Review.* Hyattsville, MD: Public Health Service.

National Highway Traffic Safety Administration (1986, September). *The economic costs to society of motor vehicle accidents.* Memorandum, Washington, D.C.: Office of Plans and Policy, National Highway Traffic Safety Administration, U.S. Department of Transportation.

Niemira, M.P. (1998). The mail-order barometer. *Chain Store Age, 74,* 40.

O'Neill, B., Lund, A. K., & Ashton, S. (1985). Mandatory belt use and driver risk taking: An empirical evaluation of the risk compensation hypothesis. In L. Evans, & R. Schwing (Eds.), *Human behavior and traffic safety* (pp. 93-107). New York: Plenum Press.

Occupational Safety and Health Administration (1999). *Draft proposed safety and health program rule.* 29 CFR 1900.1: US Department of Labor.

Pigott, H.E., Fantuzzio, J., & Gorsuch, R.L. (1987). Further generalization technology: Accounting for natural covariance in generalization assessment. *Journal of Applied Behavior Analysis, 20,* 273-278.

Poling, A., Smith, J. F., & Braatz, D. (1993). Data sets in organizational behavior management: Do we measure enough? *Journal of Organizational Behavior Management, 14,* 99-116.

Preusser, D. F., Williams, A. F., & Lund, A. K. (1985). Parental role in teenage driving. *Journal of Youth and Adolescence, 14,* 73-84.

Pritchard, R. D., Jones, S. D., Roth, P. L., Stuebing, K. K., & Ekeberg, S. E. (1988). Effects of group feedback, goal setting, and incentives on organizational productivity. *Journal of Applied Psychology (Monograph), 73,* 337-358.

Reber, R. A., & Wallin, J. A. (1984). The effects of training, goal setting, and knowledge of results on safe behavior: A component analysis. *Academy of Management Journal, 27,* 544-560.

Redmon, W. K. & Mason, M. A. (in press). Organizational Culture and Behavioral Systems Analysis. In Johnson, C. M., Redmon, W. K., & Mawhinney, T. C. (Eds.), *Organizational performance: Behavior analysis and management.* New York: The Haworth Press, Inc.

Rhoton, W. W. (1980). A procedure to improve compliance with coal mine safety regulations. *Journal of Organizational Behavior Management, 2,* 243-260.

Roberts, M. C., & Fanurik, D. (1986). Rewarding elementary school children for their use of safety-belts. *Health Psychology, 5,* 185-196.

Roberts, M.C., Fanurik, D., & Layfield, D.A. (1987). Behavioral approaches to prevention of childhood injuries. *Journal of Social Issues, 43,* 105-118.

Roberts, M. C., Fanurik, D., & Wilson, D. (1988). A community program to reward children's use of seat belts. *American Journal of Community Psychology, 16,* 395-407.

Roberts, M. C., & Layfield, D. A. (1987). Promoting child passenger safety: A comparison of two positive methods. *Journal of Pediatric Psychology, 12,* 257-271.

Roberts, M. C., & Turner, D. S. (1986). Rewarding parents for their children's use of safety seats. *Journal of Pediatric Psychology, 11,* 25-36.

Rogers-Warren, A., & Warren, S.F. (1977). *Ecological perspectives in behavior analysis.* Baltimore, MD: University Park Press.

Rudd, J. R., & Geller, E. S. (1985). A university-based incentive program to increase safety belt use: Toward cost effective institutionalization, *Journal of Applied Behavior Analysis, 18,* 215-226.

Russo, D. C., Cataldo, M. F., & Cushing, P. J. (1981). Compliance training and behavioral covariation in the treatment of multiple behavior problems. *Journal of Applied Behavior Analysis, 14,* 209-222.

Saari, J. (1987). Management of housekeeping by feedback. *Ergonomics, 30,* 313-317.

Schlinger, H., & Blakely, E. (1987). Function-altering effects of contingency-specifying stimuli. *Behavior Analyst, 10,* 41-45.

Schreuder, D. A. (1969; as cited in Wilde, 1982). *Side lights and low-beam headlights in built-up areas.* Report No. 7, SWOV, The Hague.

Schwartz, I. S., & Baer, D. M. (1991). Social validity assessments: Is current practice state of the art? *Journal of Applied Behavior Analysis, 24,* 189-204.

Short, M. S., Woelfl, G.A., & Change, C.J. (1982). Effects of traffic signal installation of accidents. *Accident prevention and analysis, 14,* 135-145.

Skinner, B.F. (1953). *Science and human behavior.* New York: Macmillan.

Skinner, B. F. (1971). *Beyond freedom and dignity.* New York: Alfred A Knopf.

Skinner, B. F. (1974). *About behaviorism.* New York: Knopf.

Sleet, D. A. (1987). Motor vehicle trauma and safety-belt use in the context of public health priorities. *The Journal of Trauma, 27,* 695-702.

Sleet, D. A., Hollenbach, K., & Hovell, M. (1986). Applying behavioral principles to motor vehicle occupant protection. *Education in Treating Children, 9,* 320-333.

Stokes, T. F., & Baer, D. M. (1977). An implicit technology of generalization. *Journal of Applied Behavior Analysis, 10,* 349-367.

Streff, F. M., & Geller, E. S. (1988). An experimental test of risk compensation: Between-subject versus within-subject analyses. *Accident Analysis and Prevention, 20,* 277-287.

Streff, F. M., Kalsher, M. J., & Geller, E. S. (1993). Developing efficient workplace safety programs: Observations of response covariation. *Journal of Organizational Behavior Management 13,* 3-14.

Stutts, J. C., Hunter, W. W., & Campbell, B. J. (1984). Three studies evaluating the effectiveness of incentives for increasing safety belt use. *Traffic Evaluation Research Review, 3,* 9-20.

Thyer, B. A., Geller, E. S., Williams, M., & Purcell, S. (1987). Community-based "flashing" to increase safety belt use. *The Journal of Experimental Education, 53,* 155-159.

Tubbs, M. E. (1987). Goal setting: A meta-analytic examination of the empirical evidence. *Journal of Applied Psychology, 71,* 474-483.

U.S. Department of Health and Human Services & Public Health Services (1991).

Healthy people 2000: National health promotion and disease prevention objectives. Special Research Report, Washington, D.C.: DHHS Publication No. (PHS) 91-50212.

Van Houten, R., & Nau, P. A. (1983). Feedback interventions and driving speed: A parametric and comparative analysis. *Journal of Applied Behavior Analysis, 16,* 253-281.

Voeltz, L. M., & Evans, I. M. (1982). The assessment of behavioral interrelationships in child behavior therpy. *Behavioral Assessment, 4,* 131-165.

Wagenaar, A. C. (1984). The economy and its effect on drinking/driving. *Abstracts and Reviews in Alcohol and Driving, 5,* 3-15.

Wahler, R. G. (1975). Some structural aspects of deviant child behavior. *Journal of Applied Behavior Analysis, 8,* 27-42.

Wahler, R. G., & Fox, J. J. (1980). Solitary toy play and time out: A family treatment package for children with aggressive and oppositional behavior. *Journal of Applied Behavior Analysis, 13,* 23-39.

Wahler, R. G., & Fox, J. J. (1981). Response structure in deviant child-parent relationships: Implications for family therapy. *Nebraska Symposium on Motivation,* 1-46.

Waller, J. A. (1987a). An overview of where we are and where we need to be. Proceedings of the 1987 Conference on Injury in America, U.S. Department of Health and Human Services, Public Health Service, *Public Health Reports, 102,* 590-591.

Waller, J. A. (1987b). Injury: Conceptual shifts and prevention implications. *Annual Review of Public Health, 8,* 21-49.

Wanchisen, B. A., & Tatham, T. A. (1991). Behavioral history: A promising challenge in explaining and controlling human operant behavior. *The Behavior Analyst, 14,* 139-144.

Warren, S. F., Baer, D. M., & Rogers-Warren, A. (1979). Teaching children to praise: A problem in stimulus and response generalization. *Child Behavior Therapy, 1,* 123-137.

Weick, K. E. (1984). Small wins: Redefining the scale of social problems. *American Psychologist, 39*(1), 40-49.

Weinberg, R. S., Bruya, L. D., & Jackson, A. (1985). The effects of goal proximity and goal specificity on endurance performance. *Journal of Sport Psychology, 7,* 296-305.

Weinstein, N. D., Grubb, P. D., & Vautier, J. S. (1986). Increasing automobile seat belt use: An intervention emphasizing risk susceptibility. *Journal of Applied Psychology, 71,* 285-290.

Wilde, G. J. S. (1982). The theory of risk homeostasis: Implications for safety and health. *Risk Analysis, 2,* 209-225.

Wilde, G. J. S., Claxton-Oldfield, S. P., & Platenius, P. H. (1985). Risk homeostasis in an experimental context. In L. Evans & R. Schwing (Eds.), *Human behavior and traffic safety* (pp. 119-149). New York: Plenum Press.

Willems, E. P. (1974). Behavioral technology and behavioral ecology. *Journal of Applied Behavior Analysis, 7,* 151-165.

Willems, E. P. (1977). Steps toward an ecobehavioral technology. In A. Rogers-Warren & S. F. Warren (Eds.), *Ecological perspectives in behavior analysis.* Baltimore, MD: University Park Press.

Winett, R. A., Moore, J. F., Wagner, J. L., Hite, L. A., Leahy, M., Neubauer, T. E., Walberg, J. L., Walker, W. B., Lombard, D., Geller, E. S., & Mundy, L. L. (1991). Altering shoppers' supermarket purchases to fit nutritional guidelines: Interactive information system. *Journal of Applied Behavior Analysis, 24,* 95-106.

Winkel, F. W. (1987). Response generalization in crime prevention campaigns: An experiment. *British Journal of Criminology, 27,* 155-173.

Wolf, M. M. (1978). Social validity: The case for subjective measurement, or how behavior analysis is finding its heart. *Journal of Applied Behavior Analysis, 11,* 203-214.

Index

Numbers in *italics* indicate figures, "t" following a page number indicates tabular material.

